Happily married
FOR A LIFETIME

Happily married
FOR A LIFETIME

Larry Koenig, PhD

Smart Family Press
11832 Newcastle Ave. Suite 3
Baton Rouge, LA 70816

www.smartdiscipline.com

1-800-255-3008
225-293-7900
225-293-7910 fax

Happilymarried
FOR A LIFETIME

by Larry Koenig, PhD

Smart Family Press
11832 Newcastle Ave. Suite 3
Baton Rouge, LA 70816
1-800-255-3008
225-293-7900
225-293-7910 fax

www.smartdiscipline.com

Cover design, interior design and production:
J Johnson Design Inc

ISBN 0-9678023-1-8

Printed and bound in the United States of America

To
Nydia

Acknowledgements

I have read the acknowledgement page of many books. Each time I have done so, I wondered why the author was thanking so many different people. It is indeed a curious thing that it takes so many people to write a book. But it does.

In writing a book, your life gets a little crazy. It takes a lot of time and concentration. To be able to manage this, you have to a lot of people around you who are willing to alter their lives in order to make it possible for you to put your full effort into writing and finishing the book.

The main person who did this for me is my wonderful wife Nydia who put up with me eating, breathing and sleeping marriage concepts. She didn't even grumble when I turned on the light and brushed my teeth at 5 A.M. every morning so I could go write. Most of all though, I want to thank Nydia for being the gracious and loving person that she is. Without my dynamic marriage to her, this book would be but a sham. And while I am on the subject I would want Nydia and everyone to know how much I appreciate her taking the time and effort in so many ways to make me feel capable, appreciated, respected, intelligent, sexy and attractive.

All kinds of other people also supported my efforts and made it possible for me to write Happily Married for a Lifetime. Andrea McLear took on the responsibility of making sure my business ran smoothly. She was aided in this task by our dedicated staff: Jennie Austin, Mark Viator, Cindy McDaniel, Christine Zoerner, Paige Weeks, Heather Dykes and Blaine Thompson. To each of these I owe a debt of gratitude for both taking on more than their share and doing a great job of it.

I especially want to thank Judy Johnson of J Johnson Design in Baton Rouge. Besides doing a spectacular job with the cover, layout and design, she is truly a marvelous person. Her encouragement, empathy and advice have been invaluable to me.

Next, I want to thank Summer Doucet for editing the book. Her skillful eye and solid advice were most appreciated as well.

Last, and so very importantly I want to thank my parents, Harold and Margaret Koenig. They have been most happily married for over sixty years. How wonderful it was to grow up with them openly expressing their love for one another in so many ways. It is my hope that their exemplary legacy of love will live on for generations to come.

Table of Contents

Introduction

Can you remember being in the honeymoon stage of your marriage? Life was bliss; you felt like the luckiest person in the world. And you were blessed with the certainty that you and your spouse would have the best marriage on earth. When you heard the words "marriage is difficult" you didn't relate; you likely even felt sorry that everyone didn't have the trouble-free relationship you and your spouse did.

Research shows that the honeymoon phase typically lasts about two years. Many couples will tell you their honeymoon ended before they got home from the trip. Perhaps you're still in the honeymoon phase. If so, enjoy every minute of it. This delightful time in a couple's relationship is both short and finite.

But why? Why can't marital bliss last forever? Wouldn't it be nice if it did? Or would it? Let's think about this for a minute: perfect relationships, perfect communication, perfect sex and perfect possessions—forever. There would be no conflict because the two of you are oblivious to any faults the other might have. What if your spouse always lovingly deferred to your every desire, your every wish? You would never argue because you'd look at one another with "goo goo" eyes and agree on everything. Your wish would be your spouse's command. How wonderful!

Or, perhaps, how terribly boring. While we might fantasize about having a spouse who lovingly supported us at every turn, we would, I think, tire of this rather quickly. Pretty soon we would become discontented with our spouse for being so darned compliant and accommodating. We would, I think, demand that our spouse start standing up to us and saying no once in a while.

And that's why marriage is so very difficult. We human beings are darned hard to satisfy. But that's the way we like it. At one time in our life we want one thing, at another time we may well want something totally different. So, our very nature as human beings causes our relationships to be difficult. But, when it comes down to it, we would have it no other way.

One thing does stay the same, though. All of us want to get all of the love out of our marriages that we can. How to do just that is the subject of this book. Within its pages you'll find information and ideas that will help you cultivate your relationship. So dive in. Pick out the ideas and exercises that feel right for you and give them a try. In so doing, it is my wish that you will get more of the love that you are seeking and that you will indeed stay "happily married for a lifetime."

How to Use This Book

The primary purpose of this book is to help people build and maintain happy and enduring marriages. The book does this in two ways: by helping couples either avoid conflicts or keep them from escalating, and by helping couples choose behaviors, strategies and solutions that will satisfy the needs of both spouses.

Throughout the book you will find strategies designed to help you avoid or successfully resolve conflicts, as well as ideas for enhancing different areas of your relationship. All the suggestions offered here are designed to help couples choose to say and do the things that result in harmony.

When perusing the book, try strategies that seem to fit your personality and relationship. If one doesn't seem comfortable to you, go on to one that does. You'll find that the ideas that appeal to you aren't necessarily ones that appeal to others, and vice versa; people vary. So, at least in the beginning, I suggest couples stick to the strategies that feel most comfortable. Later, you may want to risk a little and try some of the ideas that didn't immediately appeal to you. In doing so, you may find some suggestions that are surprisingly useful.

This is an experiential book. The more you try out the love potions suggested at the end of each segment, the more you'll get out of it. Each of the segments stands alone so you can skip around and read what interests you at the moment. All of the segments—except the first two—end with what I call "love potions," which are designed to help you get all the love you want out of your marriage. Practicing them should grow and strengthen the bond between you—and many of them are a lot of fun.

Some segments are made up strictly of questions. These segments are designed to help you get to know your partner better, which will also strengthen the bond between you. As an added bonus, they give you great practice in communicating.

The Five Principles of Harmony

Getting along: this is the biggest task of marriage. The challenge for all couples is learning how to live together harmoniously. In the beginning, it doesn't seem so tough; both husbands and wives bend over backwards to please each other. Then something happens. The stresses of living combined with the selfishness of human nature causes all kinds of conflicts, and within the first two years of marriage the focus shifts from "us" to "me." When this happens discord becomes part of the daily marriage experience.

Happily Married for a Lifetime shows you how you can return to the harmony of the early years of your love. To do so, it is helpful to first understand the principles behind harmony, what creates it and what destroys it. In the following segments you will find an explanation of each of the Principles of Harmony.

Principle Number One: People Have Needs

While much has been written about the distinct and separate needs of husbands and wives, they are really not all that different. Back it the 1960s Dr. Abraham Maslow identified five categories of needs that all people share regardless of gender. He set those needs up in a hierarchy that can be viewed as a pyramid. The physical needs are at the bottom. As these needs are fulfilled a person moves to the next level in the hierarchy. Maslow's *Hierarchy of Need* includes these five levels:

Physiological Needs: These include the things necessary for basic physical survival. They include the needs for oxygen, food, water, shelter, sex and sleep. These needs are the strongest because a person cannot survive if they are not met.

Safety Needs: These include the things necessary for a person to feel secure, stable and protected. For these needs to be satisfied, a person must be free of fear that his survival is in jeopardy.

Belonging Needs: The need to give and receive love and affection. People have an innate drive to escape from loneliness and alienation and to be an integral part of a group or family.

Esteem Needs: These need for self-respect and respect from others. In order to be happy, people must see themselves as worthy of respect and must be able to get that respect from themselves and from others. These also include a need to feel appreciated. If these needs are not met, then a person will feel worthless, weak, helpless and inferior.

Self-Actualization Needs: The need to develop and use your talents to the best of your ability in a way that benefits those around you. When a person is able to do this, she feels complete and fulfilled. If not, she feels restless, on edge, tense and somehow lacking.

People get married in order to have someone help them meet these needs. Further, people pick out a person to marry whom they best feel will be able to help them do this. When two people are in the process of deciding whether or not to marry, the ultimate decision rests on their assessments of each other's abilities to help satisfy these needs. If the assessment is positive then the marriage moves forward. If it is negative, then the individuals move on to search for someone who can better help them satisfy their needs.

Once the marriage takes place, its success is dependent on whether or not these needs are met. There is also a direct relationship between the level of happiness of the partners and the level to which they perceive their individual needs are being met. If a person believes his needs are being met for the most part, he or she is likely to be satisfied with the marriage. If both partners feel their individual needs are being met, then the marriage is perceived by both as a happy one.

It is important to realize that each person is always responsible for the fulfillment of his or her own needs; however, the Principles of Harmony recognize that married people do rely heavily on their spouses to assist in this process.

Principle Number Two: Marriage Satisfies Needs

Some needs people satisfy by themselves. Other needs we depend on our spouses to help satisfy. While people are always responsible for fulfilling their own needs, if you look at Maslow's Hierarchy of Needs you find that many are more easily met by having a marital partner.

Physiological Needs: Two people together are usually better prepared to meet the basic needs for food, shelter, sex and warmth than one person alone. It's not that a person can't provide these things alone; rather, most people assess their chances of meeting these needs as much greater with the addition of a partner. This is especially true in light of the fact that human beings know there is a likelihood that at some time they will be incapacitated and unable to provide for themselves.

Safety Needs: Security, protection and stability are often better provided by two people. This was especially true in the past as women depended on men for protection, but even today, men and women look to their partners to help satisfy their needs for stability and security. Husbands and wives help each other meet these needs through working, sharing household maintenance chores and child rearing.

Belonging Needs: Both men and women get married in part to help satisfy their needs to belong. This includes meeting needs for giving and receiving love. Certainly, people can satisfy their need to belong in many ways other than marriage, but marriage is one of the most efficacious ways of doing so. By marrying, you not only gain an instant feeling of belonging, but you are in a natural setting to give and receive love and affection on a daily basis.

Esteem Needs: Work, family members and friendships are means through which people satisfy their needs for respect and appreciation. While much has been written about self-esteem, most of a person's esteem is dependent on feedback from other people. It is out of this feedback that self-esteem grows. Through marriage a person can receive the kind of feedback that means the most; it is an environment in which a person doesn't always have to perform at a certain level to still be held in high regard. Even when a person is down and out, her mate may well provide encouragement, respect and appreciation. Knowing that someone loves you unconditionally greatly enhances a person's level of esteem and personal sense of worth.

Self-Actualization Needs: Before people can satisfy their needs to pursue and fully use their talents, they must have their other needs met. In marriages, people have mates to help them satisfy basic needs. This frees up time and energy to put into activities directed at satisfying self-actualization needs. Encouragement and moral support from a spouse can also greatly facilitate a person's setting and achieving personal and/or professional goals. Please note, as in all the need categories, it is absolutely possible for single people to satisfy their own self-actualization needs. Having a spouse, though, can help a person to do so.

In sum, at any given moment, people are involved in meeting the needs in Maslow's Hierarchy of Needs. In the case of married couples, the partners spend time meeting their own needs as well as those of their spouse.

Principle Number Three: A Dual Focus Produces Harmony

When people first fall in love and begin to court, they bend over backwards to please each other. To be sure, people watch out for their own needs, but they focus on satisfying the needs of their lovers as well. At times, each will even let the fulfillment of the other person's needs take precedence over his own needs. But, even in the early stages of love, harmony requires the needs of both people to be focused on. And with harmony, love grows.

For harmony—and thus love—to continue to grow, both people must remain aware of and take actions to satisfy their own needs as well as the needs of their partner.

Marriages stay healthy when both people have their needs met. In the best marriages, partners take responsibility for their own needs. And they take responsibility for being aware of their spouse's needs and for helping to meet them. The more often this happens, the happier a marriage becomes.

Principle Number Four: A Singular Focus Produces Discord

In marriages, when one of the partners is focused only on his or her own needs, discord is likely. This is often true in the short term and almost always true in the long term. In any given situation, if one of the spouses is only aware of and in pursuit of satisfying his own needs, conflict is not certain but likely. However, over time, if the same conditions dominate the relationship, discord is almost certain.

When it comes down to it, people will not cooperate with their spouses if their needs are not being met. They may do so in given short-term situations, but over the long term they refuse to do so. Instead, feeling that their needs are not being met, they will withdraw emotionally and often legally from the marriage.

Everyday arguments also flair up in marriages because of needs not being considered. If a person has a pinpoint focus on her own needs, conflict will result/reflect on any argument and you'll see this is true. When people feel their needs are accounted for harmony is assured; conversely, conflict occurs when they feel their needs are being either ignored or trod upon. And this normally happens when their mates are focused on meeting their own needs.

Principle Number Five: Harmony is a Choice

Even in the early stages of love, harmony results from lovers choosing to do things that will satisfy themselves as well as their partners. But it doesn't take much effort to do so because of romantic love. A large part of romantic love is made up of an acute desire to cater to the needs of the person who is at the same time catering to your own needs.

As people progress in their marriages, it gets tougher. Expectations for need fulfillment do not get met and attitudes change. People become angry, hurt and resentful. When this happens to one spouse he typically stops meeting his partner's expectations as well. To stop this cycle from destroying the marriage, choices must be consciously made and proactive plans for harmony executed.

What this means is that for harmony to exist in the long-term in a marriage, the partners must consciously choose to focus on each other's needs. Then each person must take responsibility for satisfying some of his or her own needs while also taking into account the needs of his or her spouse.

It is a fantasy to think that harmony will exist in a marriage without this kind of attention. It will not. Discord will result instead. Relationships erode over time when needs go unmet. For a marriage to flourish it is absolutely essential that the partners be proactive in becoming aware of and attending to their partner's needs as well as their own.

What is Your Love Dialect?

Dr. Gary Chapman, in his marriage program *The Five Love Languages*, points out that each person in a marriage has a favorite way of giving and receiving love. I agree. In fact, there are five distinct behaviors people engage in to communicate their love. These are: actions, attentive togetherness, physical expressions, positive strokes, and gift giving.

The idea of "love dialects" is based on several premises:

1. People give love the way they like to receive love.

2. Marriage partners rarely have the same predominant way of giving and receiving love.

3. When our partner expresses love the way we like—our "love dialect"—we feel loved.

4. When our partner expresses love to us in a different "love dialect," the effort often goes unnoticed.

Simply put, if you do not express your love in a form your spouse understands, he or she will likely fail to interpret the expression as "love."

Knowing your own love dialect will make it easier to communicate the types of things that make you feel loved, and getting to know your spouse's will help you plan the kinds of things that will make him or her feel loved. Following is a test you can take to determine your own love dialect. This can serve two purposes: first, it will tell you the ways you prefer to give and receive love; and second, it will give your spouse concrete ideas for making you feel loved.

I will repeat the test twice so both of you can take it. Try not to share your answers until both of you have finished.

Instructions: Rate each of the following statements according to how strongly you feel it represents the way you give and receive love. Use the following scale:

"1" if the statement is rarely true about the way you give and receive love

"2" if the statement is sometimes true about you

"3" if the statement is often true about you

"4" if the statement is an excellent representation of how you give and receive love

_____ 1. I feel loved when you do something I ask.

_____ 2. I feel loved when you maintain eye contact with me while I am talking.

_____ 3. I love it when you ask me for a hug.

_____ 4. When you compliment me I feel especially loved.

_____ 5. I love it when you bring me gifts.

_____ 6. When you jump in to help me do things, I really appreciate it.

_____ 7. I need to spend some time "really" talking with you every day.

_____ 8. I wish you would kiss me more often.

_____ 9. Compliments go a long way with me.

_____ 10. I especially like it when you surprise me with little gifts.

_____ 11. I often comment to other people about how much you help me get things done.

_____ 12. It doesn't really matter what we're doing; I just enjoy being with you.

_____ 13. I could enter "the longest kissing contest" with you and enjoy every minute.

_____ 14. When you say nice things about me, it is music to my ears.

_____ 15. What I look forward to more than anything is giving and receiving gifts.

_____ 16. When I want to express my love, I first think of what I might do special for you.

_____ 17. I think the best way to spell love is T-I-M-E.

_____ 18. I wish we would hug and cuddle more often.

_____ 19. More than anything, I think it's important to say "I love you" at least once a day.

_____ 20. I spend a lot of time picking out gifts. After all, the perfect gift is a great way to say "I love you."

_____ 21. The more things you do for me, the more I feel loved.

_____ 22. More than anything, I look forward to the time we spend together.

_____ 23. To tell you the truth, the way to my heart is through physical expressions of love.

_____ 24. I absolutely love writing and receiving little "love notes."

_____ 25. If I were rich, I would buy you a gift every day.

_____ 26. I constantly look for ways to do things for you. That is how I express my love best.

_____ 27. You can tell how much I love you just by how much time I spend doing things with you.

_____ 28. If you want to show me how much you love me, then you will be wonderfully affectionate.

_____ 29. You can count on me to give you lots of appreciation and praise.

_____ 30. Whenever I'm feeling especially loving, I start looking for a gift to give you.

Now go back and add 3 to the two statements you feel most accurately describe the way you give and receive love. Then transfer your answers to the answer sheet on the following page.

Love Dialect Scoring Sheet

Transer your answers to the blanks below (the numbers below correspond to the numbers of the questions you answered). You will find this an easy task if you go across the rows of the blanks below. Be sure to add in the points for the statements you felt most strongly represent the way you give and receive love.

After you transfer your answers, add the columns up and record the total at the bottom. The highest score will represent the way in which you best like to give and receive love.

Actions	Attentive Togetherness	Physical Expressions	Positive Strokes	Gift Giving
1._____	2._____	3._____	4._____	5._____
6._____	7._____	8._____	9._____	10._____
11._____	12._____	13._____	14._____	15._____
16._____	17._____	18._____	19._____	20._____
21._____	22._____	23._____	24._____	25._____
26._____	27._____	28._____	29._____	30._____
Totals _____	_____	_____	_____	_____

Your Primary Love Dialect is _____

Your Secondary Love Dialect is _____

_____ 1. I feel loved when you do something I ask.

_____ 2. I feel loved when you maintain eye contact with me while I am talking.

_____ 3. I love it when you ask me for a hug.

_____ 4. When you compliment me I feel especially loved.

_____ 5. I love it when you bring me gifts.

_____ 6. When you jump in to help me do things, I really appreciate it.

_____ 7. I need to spend some time "really" talking with you every day.

_____ 8. I wish you would kiss me more often.

_____ 9. Compliments go a long way with me.

_____ 10. I especially like it when you surprise me with little gifts.

_____ 11. I often comment to other people about how much you help me get things done.

_____ 12. It doesn't really matter what we're doing; I just enjoy being with you.

_____ 13. I could enter "the longest kissing contest" with you and enjoy every minute.

_____ 14. When you say nice things about me, it is music to my ears.

_____ 15. What I look forward to more than anything is giving and receiving gifts.

_____ 16. When I want to express my love, I first think of what I might do special for you.

_____ 17. I think the best way to spell love is T-I-M-E.

_____ 18. I wish we would hug and cuddle more often.

_____ 19. More than anything, I think it's important to say "I love you" at least once a day.

_____ 20. I spend a lot of time picking out gifts. After all, the perfect gift is a great way to say "I love you."

_____ 21. The more things you do for me, the more I feel loved.

_____ 22. More than anything, I look forward to the time we spend together.

_____ 23. To tell you the truth, the way to my heart is through physical expressions of love.

_____ 24. I absolutely love writing and receiving little "love notes."

_____ 25. If I were rich, I would buy you a gift every day.

_____ 26. I constantly look for ways to do things for you. That is how I express my love best.

_____ 27. You can tell how much I love you just by how much time I spend doing things with you.

_____ 28. If you want to show me how much you love me, then you will be wonderfully affectionate.

_____ 29. You can count on me to give you lots of appreciation and praise.

_____ 30. Whenever I'm feeling especially loving, I start looking for a gift to give you.

Now go back and add 3 to the two statements you feel most accurately describe the way you give and receive love. Then transfer your answers to the answer sheet on the following page.

Love Dialect Scoring Sheet

Transer your answers to the blanks below (the numbers below correspond to the numbers of the questions you answered). You will find this an easy task if you go across the rows of the blanks below. Be sure to add in the points for the statements you felt most strongly represent the way you give and receive love.

After you transfer your answers, add the columns up and record the total at the bottom. The highest score will represent the way in which you best like to give and receive love.

Actions	Attentive Togetherness	Physical Expressions	Positive Strokes	Gift Giving
1._____	2._____	3._____	4._____	5._____
6._____	7._____	8._____	9._____	10._____
11._____	12._____	13._____	14._____	15._____
16._____	17._____	18._____	19._____	20._____
21._____	22._____	23._____	24._____	25._____
26._____	27._____	28._____	29._____	30._____
Totals _____	_____	_____	_____	_____

Your Primary Love Dialect is _____

Your Secondary Love Dialect is _____

How to Speak Your Spouse's Love Dialect

Now that you know your spouse's dialect, you will want to put this information to use. The more ways you express your love according to your spouse's love dialect, the more your spouse will feel loved. And the more loved your spouse feels, the more he or she will want to reciprocate.

Following are the five love dialects and suggested types of loving behaviors for each. Talk them over with your spouse, put a check by the ones that appeal to you most and add other suggestions in the blanks provided.

Actions

If your mate's primary love dialect is Actions, you will want to express your love through:

1. household chores
2. household maintenance
3. special projects
4. yard work
5. remodeling
6. doing the dishes
7. helping children with homework
8. doing laundry
9. helping with elderly parents
10. grocery shopping
11. other acts of kindness

12. _____

13. _____

14. _____

15. _____

Attentive Togetherness

If your spouse's love dialect is Attentive Togetherness, you will want to express your love through:

1. sitting and talking
2. going out to eat, just the two of you, for a romantic dinner
3. going for long walks together
4. going on picnics
5. going shopping together
6. going antique hunting together
7. taking up a sport together
8. taking up a hobby together
9. reading out loud to one another
10. worshiping together
11. attending sporting events together
12. _____
13. _____
14. _____
15. _____

Physical Expressions

If your spouse's love dialect is Physical Expressions, you will want to express your love through:

1. hugs

2. kissing

3. making love (with lots of foreplay)

4. holding hands

5. blowing kisses

6. wrestling

7. tickling

8. making "goo goo" eyes

9. massages

10. cuddling

11. spooning

12. _____

13. _____

14. _____

15. _____

Positive Strokes

If your spouse's love dialect is Positive Strokes, you will want to express your love through:

1. love notes strategically hidden to be found throughout the day

2. complimenting clothes

3. complimenting hair

4. compliment physical attributes

5. expressing gratitude for doing ordinary things like house or yard work

6. expressing appreciation for listening and understanding

7. expressing appreciation for taking care of children or working

8. saying "I love you" morning, noon and night

9. buying special greeting cards

10. writing poetry expressing your love

11. writing love letters

12. _____

13. _____

14. _____

15. _____

Receiving Gifts

If your spouse's love dialect is Receiving Gifts, you will want to express your love through:

1. giving small surprise gifts

2. ending flowers

3. buying candy

4. shopping together at the mall

5. buying birthday presents

6. buying lots of Christmas presents

7. wrapping the gifts beautifully

8. making opening gifts a special event and/or big production

9. taking pictures of the gift-opening event

10. giving gifts for "no particular reason"

11. hiding gifts under his or her pillow

12. _____

13. _____

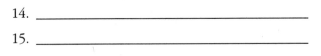
14. _____

15. _____

Love Potion #1

Surprise your spouse at least once a week for the next month with some expression of love that fits his or her love dialect. Make it something as special as possible. Also, remember to express appreciation when your spouse expresses love to you in your love dialect.

The Most Common Method of Motivating Change in a Marriage

During the honeymoon phase, lovers are mostly blinded to each other's faults. In short, they see their partner as "perfect." When asked if there is anything he or she would change about the other, the answer is normally a loving, "No, Sweetheart. Don't change a thing. I love you just the way you are."

Of course, once the "honeymoon" is over, it's another story. The blinders come off and the flaws are revealed. What a shock this can be! For some, it can be like parking a shiny brand new car out in the grocery store parking lot and coming out to find it all dented up. For others, it's a slower process in which the awareness of flaws dawns on them over a period of years. But the result is the same. What was once flawless is now viewed as damaged goods.

In some respects, it's almost worse than this. I say this because we tend to view faults as being under the conscious control of our partner. At first they're pointed out with great care and kindness with a request for change, something like: "Darling, I love you so much. Can I tell you something without you getting mad? I can? Well, I know it's a small thing and I don't want to nit pick, but would you mind keeping your dirty socks off the kitchen table?"

No matter what the immediate response, be it positive or negative, the person tends not to change. Habits, we all know, are extremely difficult to break. So, in the given scenario, the offender absentmindedly goes right back to leaving his socks on the kitchen table. Now the couple is on a track to conflict.

Repeated offenses are now met with criticism—the most common method of motivating change in a marriage. Criticism is based on two assumptions. The first assumption is that our partner is oblivious to his faults and therefore needs them to be pointed out. The second assumption is that the criticism needs to be harsh in order to motivate the person to change.

Based on these assumptions, the complaining partner, angry now that her request for change is being ignored, ends up saying something like, "Do you know what your problem is? No? Then let me tell you. You're the messiest person I've ever met. And you have no regard for my needs whatsoever. I'm tired of always having to pick up after you. If you really loved me, you would change!"

Insight plus motivation. This would seem to be a good thing. But it isn't. The problem here is that criticism destroys relationships. It destroys relationships because of our nature as human beings.

Human beings will not remain in a positive relationship with someone who is always critical. We simply will not do it. Instead, we will do one of two things: either we will get away from the person, or, if we feel trapped, we will try to make that person as miserable as he or she is making us with the criticism.

Couples cannot afford to get into a cycle of criticism. Millions of couples have lousy relationships, and many of them got that way through well-intended criticism. The good news is that there are also millions of couples out there that have wonderful and happy relationships. But they've learned to handle their spouse's faults much differently. The chapter after next discusses the positive ways successful couples handle faults; the next chapter looks at some of the other maladaptive ways people in marriages deal with conflict.

Love Potion #2

Go to a movie. After the movie, go somewhere for a snack and pick out two couples each to discuss—one couple you know whose relationship you admire and another couple whose marriage you think is headed for the divorce courts. Discuss why you think each couple has a great or a lousy marriage.

Add to this discussion your views on criticism. Answer the question, "Is constructive criticism okay?" If so, "What is the difference between constructive and destructive criticism?"

Other Dysfunctional Strategies for Resolving Differences

The ability to resolve conflicts is a prerequisite for a happy and stable marriage. It is also one of the most difficult tasks of the marital relationship. It takes a lot of effort to become adept at resolving differences in a mature and healthy fashion. This is why couples often try to get what they want by employing one of the following strategies:

1. Anger

2. Defensiveness, making excuses

3. Withdrawing physically

4. Revenge

5. Sarcasm

6. Contempt

7. Put downs

8. Guilt trips

9. Violence

10. Placating

11. Stonewalling

12. Cross-complaining

13. Yes-butting

14. Whining

15. Broken Record Syndrome

16. Denying responsibility

17. Blaming

18. Drinking

19. Taking drugs

20. Throwing-in-the-kitchen-sink

21. Making threats

22. Escaping (all kinds: television, books, computers, friends, sleeping, etc.)

23. Rubber Man/Rubber Woman Syndrome

24. Lying

25. Sulking

26. Poor Me Syndrome

27. Pushing buttons

28. Complaining incessantly

29. Refusing to cooperate

30. Throwing a temper tantrum

Only two of these may need explanation. Throwing-in-the-kitchen-sink is when an argument starts and one or both of the participants bring up every wrong thing the other person did that they can think of, both past and present. The Rubber Man/Rubber Woman Syndrome is when one person has a complaint and the other simply voices the same complaint back. For example: "You never listen to me!" followed by "Well, you never listen to me either!"

None of the above takes any practice. All of us have at one time or another dealt with our conflicts in one or several of these rather dysfunctional ways. One of the worst things we can do is enforce the use of these devices by giving in to someone who employs them. If the strategies are enforced, they will be used over and over again until the marriage can't stand it any longer.

There are so many negative ways to respond to conflict that it's no wonder couples have so much trouble solving problems. Added to this is the fact that most of us learned how to get what we wanted by watching and copying our parents' behavior. Though intellectually we may look at the way our parents resolved conflicts and recognize what was good and what was bad, we end up repeating the maladaptive behaviors anyway.

Couples who wish to live happily together must find both healthy ways to resolve conflict and adaptive ways of negotiating for what they want.

Love Potion #3

Individually go over the list and admit to yourself which of the dysfunctional strategies you employ to either get your way or resolve conflicts. Pledge to yourself that you will not use these methods for the next week. Resolve instead to use some of the functional strategies described in the upcoming chapters. Now, go surprise your spouse with something nice.

How to Resolve Conflict the Easiest Way

As I said in a previous chapter, being able to successfully deal with and resolve conflict is a prerequisite for a long and happy marriage. In the last chapter I suggested why it's so difficult to resolve conflict and deal with differences. In this chapter I offer the first of several ways that you can resolve conflict and get more of what you want out of your marriage.

When it comes down to it, resolving conflict and getting what you want are very much the same tasks. What I mean is this: conflict comes about because of dissatisfaction; dissatisfaction comes about because we are not getting what we want; ergo, resolving conflict becomes a process of learning how to get what you want. Of course, in a marriage you want to do this in a way that preserves the love between you and your spouse.

Following is the easiest and most functional way of getting what you want in your relationship. It's a two-step process.

First, it's necessary to decide what you want. This isn't all that hard if you stop and think about it. We know what we want, but we aren't always good at defining just what it is in a way that we can communicate it to another person. So, the first thing to do is to take a pad and pencil and write down what you want. If at first you read what you've written and find it to be either unclear or unsatisfying, write it again and again until you are satisfied with it.

Once you're clear on what you want, ask your spouse for it. Do not justify it in any way; simply ask for what you want. But do make sure to ask with a positive attitude and a positive expectation that you will get it.

Requests can be simple or complex. They might include:

1. Would you please help me fold the laundry?

2. Would you please help me paint the fence?

3. Would you please watch the kids on Thursday nights so I can take a Karate class?

4. Would you please go out to diner and a movie with me on Friday night?

5. Would you please go to the doctor and take care or your snoring problem?

6. Would you please pick your socks up?

7. Would you mind if I went fishing with my friends on Saturday?

8. Can we set a time when we can talk over some issues that have been bothering me?

9. Would you please have sex with me tonight?

10. Would you please take me out on Saturday evening?

Simple requests can work wonders. It's important here to remember to only make the request. Leave off the reasons why. Just make the direct request.

For many people, making simple requests is very difficult. However, simple clear requests are the easiest way to get what you want. They're also the most functional way of resolving conflicts. Often, rather than get into a big fight over how your spouse never does what you want, you can avoid the fight altogether by simply asking for what you want. If you can do this and not fire any shots in the process, you're much more likely to get what you want while avoiding a conflict.

Some people object to this process because they have one of two negative attitudes about asking. One of these goes like this: "Why should I have to ask? My spouse knows what needs to be done and he/she should just go ahead and do it without my having to ask." Another of these attitudes goes like this: "Why should I have to ask my spouse for anything? I'm an adult now and I should be able to do whatever I want without having to ask." The answer to both of these is the same. If you ask for what you want, you will get more of what you want, you will avoid conflict, and you will likely preserve your marriage.

Of course, it's possible your spouse will say no. But you'll get more of what you want if you ask with the attitude that your spouse has every right to say no to you. If your spouse does say no, say something like, "I respect your right to say no and I'll bet you have some good reasons for saying no. Would you tell me what they are?

Sometimes, if you can respond non-defensively when someone says no, he'll change his mind almost immediately. I think this is because often we're programmed to say no automatically even when we have little or no reason to do so.

If this doesn't get you what you want and you're still determined to achieve your goal, try some of the other strategies in the up-coming chapters on resolving conflict.

Love Potion #4

Make a list of the issues you normally fight about. From that list make another list of some of the things you want your spouse to do. Pick four things off the list and ask for one of them each week for a month. If you find you have trouble asking for what you want, read Mark Victor Hansen and Jack Canfield's book, *The Aladdin Factor*. It is an absolutely wonderful book about how to ask for and get what you want. This is also a great book to read if you want to increase your level of success in your career. Now go ask your spouse for a bear hug.

Where Does Your Marriage Fit In?

According to a study of 15,000 couples done at the University of Minnesota, there are seven different kinds of marriages. As reported in *Spectrum NewsMagazine*, these included the following.

Instructions: Read the following out loud to your spouse. Discuss which category your marriage likely fits. Also talk about where you would like it to be.

1. **Devitalized:** These couples described themselves as very unhappy with all aspects of their relationships. This group has a high likelihood of divorce and comprises 40% of all marriages.

2. **Financially:** Focused: In these marriages the couple's careers come before the relationship. Money, not love, is what holds the marriage together. This group accounts for 14% of all marriages.

3. **Conflicted:** These couples are quite dissatisfied with a number of facets of their marriage but not all. Conflicts are often left unresolved and pleasure is sought outside the relationship. This group also accounts for 14% of all marriages.

4. **Traditional:** These marriages are better off, with the couple reporting satisfaction in a number of areas. However, communication problems and difficulties with sex are frequent complaints. 10% of marriages fit into this category.

5. **Balanced:** These couples say they're moderately satisfied with their marriages. They tend to be strong in problem-solving and communication, but money is often a recurring problem. 8% of couples belong to this category.

6. **Harmonious:** Highly satisfied couples make up this category. They are very satisfied with each other but often complain about the children. If there are any problems or difficulties it's normally with the children. This group accounts for 8% of the marriages.

7. **Vitalized:** The couples in this category are also very satisfied spouses and their marriages. In addition, they have strong internal resources and are very good at resolving conflicts. 6% of marriages fall into this category.

Love Potion #5

Go out and buy some massage lotion and some scented candles. Give your spouse a surprise massage tonight.

Good Marriages Have One Cheerleader, Great Marriages Have Two

"Behind every successful man is a woman!" It's been a cliché for years, and like most clichés it's been around for so long because it's true.

In one of my books, *Smart Discipline for the Classroom,* I point out to teachers that success is dependent on encouragement, and that students cannot be successful in school unless they have someone to encourage them.

This also applies to marriages. In highly satisfying marriages, both partners encourage the other's hopes, dreams and aspirations. And they do it on a daily basis for years. Encouragement becomes a habit.

Being your partner's greatest supporter is easy if you are either still in the honeymoon phase of your marriage or if you agree whole-heartedly with your spouse's plans. The difficulty arises when you either don't agree with his or her aspirations or think your spouse is being anything from unrealistic to out-and-out stupid.

Of course, when people share their plans with someone else, they often get caught up in their own excitement. At this time, they're very open and vulnerable. They're risking their inner most dreams and ideas by sharing them with another person.

The other person, at this point, has several choices. One choice is to support and encourage, another is to listen and clarify, and another is to discourage. The first two choices strengthen relationships and the third destroys.

"Destroy" may seem a bit too strong, but it's a very real and major risk you take when you impede another's dreams. Even if you're right and the dream could never come true in a million years, the last thing you want to do to your spouse is point out why his idea won't work. In doing so, you will likely dissuade him from the dream—but at the same time you'll bruise your relationship badly. Do it enough times and you'll likely destroy it.

So what do you do when your spouse has a crazy idea and you're afraid she's about to "bet the farm" and lose it? The first thing to do is listen and clarify. Enthusiastically as you can, ask all kinds of questions. Be interested and show that you understand how excited your partner is about her ideas. Say things like, "It sure seems like you're excited about this. Tell me more about it." And "Oh really, tell me more. What would you do then?"

What we need most as human beings is to have someone listen to and understand us. When you give the gift of understanding and listening, you really do not have to fear what your mate will do with the idea at hand. Most likely, if it actually is a dumb idea, he'll realize this on his own within several days. Life has a way of throwing major hurdles up to dash crazy ideas before they get off the ground.

If this happens, and you've supported your spouse, she'll always remember and appreciate that support. If, on the other hand, your spouse does start to embark on an endeavor that you cannot support, you're in a much better position to say no if you've taken the time to fully understand the idea in the first. Your spouse will appreciate you for listening and will now likely be open to listening to your thoughts on the subject.

But be careful with this. Encouragement or the lack thereof has a major bearing on the quality of a love relationship. For the most part, if you establish a habit of actively encouraging your spouse, you can look forward to a good deal of return encouragement. As well, you will likely have a spouse who'll achieve much greater things than he would have without your support.

Encouragement is an elixir of love. Give it in great measure and your love will grow accordingly. Withhold it and your love will diminish accordingly. It is truly your choice. Remember this, too: whether you choose to encourage or discourage your spouse, he or she will always remember it!

Love Potion #6

Buy tickets to an event you know your spouse would enjoy. Tell your spouse that you have the tickets but do not tell him/her what event they are for. Joke about the upcoming event but keep it a complete surprise. The anticipation should be as fun as the event itself!

How to Establish a Positive Vision for Your Marriage

In my work with people over the years, I've found that one of the chief reasons why people don't get what they want out of life is that they don't have a clear idea of what they want in the first place. This is just as true in marriages. If you do not have a crystal clear idea of what's important to you in your marriage, you will probably end up dissatisfied.

Knowing this, a couple seeking a long and happy marriage would be wise to take some time to establish a joint vision for their marriage. Here's how:

Step One: Set aside about an hour when you can spend some time uninterrupted. Turn off the television and agree to let the answering machine take messages. Fix yourself some snacks and put on some romantic music. Get out some paper and pencils.

Step Two: Separately, on a sheet of paper write positive statements about your marriage. Some examples are: "We are best friends"; "We are wonderfully affectionate"; "We like the same foods"; and "We have passionate sex." Be sure to make each statement affirmative—instead of writing something like, "We don't put each other down," say, "We support and encourage each other."

Step Three: Add to your list positive statements that you would like to be true about your marriage. State them in the same way you stated the ones you already feel are true. In other words, write them in the present tense, like: "We love to go dancing together." You can brainstorm the things you want on this list or choose from some of the following:

1. We are openly affectionate

2. We are good at resolving conflicts

3. We have positive attitudes

4. We are both totally committed to making this marriage work

5. We have strong communication skills

6. We are very considerate of each other

7. We are good at solving problems together

8. We are creative

9. We are financially organized and responsible

10. We are flexible in our thinking

11. We are best friends

12. We are generous

13. We love to give gifts to each other

14. We are honest with each other

15. We both do our fair share of household duties

16. We are good at listening to each other

17. We are great in the love-making department

18. We are patient with each other

19. We love to play together

20. We are a romantic couple

21. We have a high degree of awareness about our relationship

22. We share laughter and delight on a daily basis

23. We are sensitive to each other's needs

24. We are spontaneous with each other

Step Four: Share your list with your spouse. Put checks by the ones you have in common. Add statements from your spouse's list that you agree with but don't have on your list.

Step Five: Go back individually and put an X by the ones that are most important to you. Choose about seven items.

Step Six: Take a clean sheet of paper, get together with your spouse, and make one list. Be sure to include all seven items from each of your lists.

Step Seven: Put the list up somewhere you can't help but notice and read it on a daily basis.

One of the most powerful ways of getting what you want out of life is to define what you want and write it down. I don't know why this is, but there is almost something magical about writing down your goals. I can't recommend the completion of this exercise highly enough!

Love Potion #7

Make some love coupons to give your spouse. Go back to the test on Love Dialects that your spouse took and make a love coupon for every way that he/she likes to receive love. Put them in an envelope and put the envelope in your spouse's pillowcase.

What Makes Up a Happy Marriage?

People have different ideas about what makes a happy marriage. But, for many, the question is one that they have not asked themselves. Or at least if they have, they don't have a definitive answer in mind. So I think it is worthwhile to look at how other people define a happy marriage.

Judith Wallerstein and Sandra Blakeslee undertook the task of interviewing successful couples across America to find out how people define a happy marriage. They report their results in a wonderful book called *The Good Marriage*. Here are the types of things they found that go into the making of a happy marriage.

1. Respect between the partners

2. Each person cherishes the other

3. Each person likes the other

4. Both find pleasure and comfort it the other's company

5. Emotional support of each other

6. Mutually satisfying physical intimacy

7. An expression of appreciation between the partners

8. The creation of fond memories

9. A feeling of safety, friendship and trust

10. A feeling that the spouse is central to their world

11. An admiration of positive qualities such as honesty, generosity, decency, loyalty and fairness

12. A strong sense of morality

13. The conviction that each person is worthy of being loved

14. A sense of reality, in that there are some problems but that they are surmountable

15. A view that each partner is special in some important regard

16. A sense that the marriage enhances each partner

17. The sense that there is a unique fit between each partner's needs and his or her spouse's willingness and ability to meet those needs

18. The sense that each partner is lucky to have the other

19. An equitable division of household tasks and child-rearing

20. A sense that success of the marriage was attributable to both partners

21. An ability to express both positive and negative emotions

22. A shared view that the marriage took constant attention and work

This is quite a list, isn't it? Surely any couple who has these things has a wonderful marriage. They are indeed very blessed as well.

However, it is important to note that a marriage such as this does not come about by accident. It takes years of dedicated work to bring this kind of relationship into existence. The good news is that it is certainly doable; in fact, there are millions of couples in America who have just this kind of relationship. It does, though, take a major commitment on both parts to continually work on the relationship.

While I say that it takes a commitment from both people, please know that at any point in time the task of keeping the relationship together may fall to one person or the other. At the time, it may seem unfair. But that's the way relationships are. Sometimes one of the partners goes through a period of intense personal challenge, severely hampering his or her ability to contribute to the marriage. During these times, if the marriage is to survive, it is up to the partner to keep the relationship together.

These are dangerous times in a relationship, dangerous in the sense that one person can come to feel so over-burdened by the problems that he or she decides to end the relationship. Even the person facing personal challenges may decide that he or she would be better off if the marriage ended. Some even come to think that the partner is the cause of the problems.

If marriages are to survive long enough to cultivate the wonderful characteristics listed earlier in this chapter, then both partners must agree to stick with the marriage until the current challenges can be met and overcome. The pay-off comes in the long run, when surviving the rough times eventually strengthens the marriage. In a way, it's like a bone that breaks. When it heals, the fracture becomes the strongest part of the bone. So too can it be in a marriage. Once overcome, the trouble may well become a source of strength to the marriage.

In sum, your marriage can become one of great satisfaction and enduring love. But it will take lots of work and a commitment to staying in the marriage even through the rough times.

Love Potion #8

On a copy machine, make two copies of the list at the beginning of this chapter. Working separately, circle the items that you strongly feel already exist in your marriage. Put an X by the ones you feel need work. Discuss your results and brainstorm ways to work on the areas needing attention. Make a list of these things. Then pick 3 things off the list that each of you would be willing to do differently to improve your marriage. They can be different things and the selection should be totally up to each individual. As each of you put your chosen items into action, make sure to give your partner lots of appreciation. Express some appreciation right now.

The Essential Tasks of Building a Good Marriage

Drawing from the research of Dr. Judith Wallerstein in her book *The Good Marriage*, there are nine psychological tasks that couples must accomplish if they are to build a lasting and happy marriage. While these tasks are not imposed by anyone else, they are necessary to the health of a marital relationship. To not successfully undertake and complete these tasks is to put the relationship on a course toward failure.

The first task is for the partners to commit to each other and at the same time detach themselves emotionally from their families of origin. In so doing they must come to relate as a couple to their now extended families so that they can form their own unique family. During this time the partners help one another complete their transition into adulthood.

The second challenge or task is to build a sense of "us" through intimacy while at the same time figuring out an area of autonomy. Building the relationship into a cohesive unit is the major challenge of this task, with both partners reaching agreement and feeling good about the new partnership. However, tricky as it may be, both people in the new union must also figure out for themselves how they can maintain their individuality.

In the third task of marriage the couple faces bringing children into the family and the challenges of parenting. While having children is one of the most binding and satisfying tasks of the marriage, the real challenge comes in nurturing the relationship at the same time that you nurture the children.

Managing the unpredictable adversities of life is the fourth task of marriage. Crisis- or stress-management is the name of the game. Life inevitably brings with it illnesses, job loss, relocations, natural disasters and deaths of family and friends. Despite the anguish these events can bring, the couple must learn how to get through them in a way that strengthens their love.

Next on the list of tasks is to figure out how to handle conflict, anger and differences between the partners. The challenge here is to confront these issues in a way that each person feels safe and cared for. For each to feel secure expressing anger and individual desires, both partners must reject all uses of physical and emotional abuse. Instead, functional ways of settling differences must be learned.

Establishing a mutually satisfying sex life is the sixth task of marriage. While this would seem the easiest of the tasks, it isn't. A sex life that meets the needs of both partners takes time, love and sensitivity. This task is made more daunting by the influences of stress and hormonal changes at different times in the partners' lives. Because of these influences, much care must go into developing and maintaining a good sexual relationship.

The sharing of laughter and delight is the seventh task of marriage. Playfulness is an essential ingredient for a vital marital relationship. Just as learning to handle the tough times in a marriage is critical, it is just as important to have fun together. The ability to have fun together is what can keep the marriage alive and vibrant.

The eighth task is to learn how to encourage each other and to provide the nurturing that the other needs. Accomplishing this task strengthens the bond of love between the partners and is absolutely essential to a good marriage.

To accomplish the ninth task, couples must develop and recall a positive history of their togetherness. They must come to recall together the wonderful romantic and passionate times of their early relationship and use them to foster present day romantic experiences. However, these recollections and desires to recreate the emotions and experiences in the present day must be tempered with reality and the changes that time has wrought.

Any couple who is able to meet these challenges and accomplish these tasks is sure to have a strong and vibrant marriage. In the following pages you will find information, suggestions and exercises that will help you accomplish these tasks so you can be happily married for a lifetime.

Love Potion #9

Either cook your spouse's favorite meal or take him/her out to eat at his/her favorite restaurant. Make it a surprise!

The Seven Stages of Marriage and How to Meet the Predictable Challenges of Each

Maxine Rock, in her book *The Marriage Map*, identifies seven stages of marriage. Following is a description of each of the stages. Much of what this book is about is how to meet the challenges of these stages.

It is important to know that there are stages in marriage. Knowing this allows us to realize that we are not alone in the challenges we are facing, and that each phase will indeed pass if we have the patience to hang in there.

Stage one is the honeymoon period. During this phase of marriage, the couple derives intense satisfaction from the relationship. Each partner is blind to the other's faults, or either minimizes or dismisses them as trivial. Emotionally and sexually the couple is on a natural high. The average length of this period of marriage is two years. Some report their honeymoon ended before they got home from the trip; others say their honeymoon lasted several years.

Stage two is the compromise period. In this stage of marriage, the blinders come off and each partner becomes acutely aware of the other's faults. What a disappointment it can be to find out your partner is far from the perfect person you thought you married. Some of the faults annoy, others seem hurtful. The couple, during this stage, starts to negotiate change. Couples that successfully make it through the compromise stage both ask for change and agree to do some changing themselves. Others, faced with all their partner's faults as well as being confronted by their own faults, decide to flee the marriage. This stage normally lasts between two and seven years.

Stage three is the period of reality struggles. Reality sets in during this stage of marriage. While the couple has negotiated for and gotten some change, each partner realizes that the other is basically "who they are" and is unlikely to change significantly. This is also the time when more bonding takes place, as the partners come to accept each other, blemishes and all. Having children and financial dependence also serve to strengthen the marital bonds during this stage. This normally represents the fifth to the tenth years of marriage.

Stage four is called the time of decisions. Having come to face that each marriage partner has his or her faults, ongoing decisions have to be made as to whether or not each person can continue in the marriage given the other's faults. At this point, the partners start to weigh the other's good points against his or her faults. They question whether or not the positive points of their mate makes it worth putting up with the bad. This stage usually occupies the tenth to the fifteenth years of marriage.

Stage five is called separation. This is a time when partners push away from each other. Some divorce, some separate and others distance themselves emotionally from their partners. This stage of marriage is extremely painful. The stage ends when and if the couples enter into discussions on what changes each want and are willing to make in order to make the marriage work. Given the willingness to engage in this process the love grows and strengthens.

Those that last through the first five stages of marriage enter into the sixth stage which is called together again. In this stage the couple comes to final terms with their differences and decides to live with them no matter what. Talk of divorce or separation is normally set aside in favor of realization that this union is for life. Chance for love and growth in the marriage are greatly enhanced when this decision is reached. Attentions now turn to enhancing the marriage and committing to the long-term. This stage usually occupies the seventeenth to the twentieth years of marriage.

Stage seven is called new freedom. Couples in this stage breathe a sigh of relief. They no longer have to pour so much energy into changing or making the marriage work. They enter into a natural flow of being together. Neither worries much any more about what the other is thinking or doing. Trust, compassion, communication and support flow freely between the partners. This is also a time when the partners, secure in their marriages, explore new ways of fulfilling themselves. This stage, which normally occupies the twentieth to twenty-fifth years of marriage, is considered by many as the beginning of the best years of marriage.

Last comes what is called ongoing growth. This is not a stage, as it has no end. Rather, it is a time in the marriage when the couple has successfully completed the stages and now is free to expand both their love and personal horizons. It is the time when both can relax and enjoy each other and their lives. This is the rich reward for sticking out the tough times and keeping the marriage together.

According to Maxine Rock every marriage goes through these stages, no exceptions. However, if it is a remarriage, couples quickly go through the initial stages and catch up to where they left off in the previous marriage. The stages then progress at a normal rate. If you get married when you're older, you quickly catch up to your peers' relationships and then progress at a normal rate.

Love Potion #10

Read the stages out loud to your partner when you are driving somewhere. Discuss which stages you have gone through and what stage you think your marriage is in now. Discuss why you think it is helpful to know about the stages of marriage. When you stop the car make out with your spouse for at least two minutes.

The Art of Settling Arguments: Part One

Conflicts come up in all marriages. They simply cannot be avoided. Even before getting married, couples start to have spats over jealousy and in-law issues. After they get married they move on to arguments that arise over sex and communication. Then come arguments over the handling of household tasks and children.

At every turn in the first twenty years of marriage there are all types of arguments that crop up in marriages. The subjects change but the thing that remains constant is the need to deal with conflicts in ways that both resolve the problem and preserve the marriage.

Most couples come to a conflict resolution style through trial and error. This is not so much by choice or design but rather because they are not presented with any other ways to learn problem-solving. If they were, I suppose many would opt to learn the art of settling arguments peacefully. Wouldn't you? If so, you will be interested in this chapter.

The first skill to be learned in the art of settling arguments is both the easiest and the most difficult one. This is the skill of listening. On the one hand, listening is extremely easy. All it takes is for one person to be quiet, be attentive, look at the person who is talking, ask pertinent questions and clarify what the other person is saying. This is an easy process and one that takes little training to learn.

What make listening difficult are the emotions we feel. Often in marital communication, the person talking will say his or her peace and the person listening will become highly defensive and angry over what was said. This is a major problem, because for any argument to be resolved successfully there must be a discussion of the issues. Both parties must be able to clearly state their position and feel that the other person has listened and understood.

If each person can state his or her position and end up feeling heard and understood, resolving the problem will likely be much easier. In fact, between seventy and eighty percent of all arguments can be resolved if this process can be successfully completed without any action having to be taken. The reason for this is because one of the largest human needs each person has is to be listened to and understood. So large is this need that in America we spend billions of dollars every year to hire people to listen to us. We call them psychologists, social workers, counselors, ministers and therapists. Why do we pay them so much? Well, because we have a deep need to be listened to and understood, yet we do not have people in our family who are willing or able to do so.

When it comes down to it, if partners can learn how to listen to each other, they can and will likely have a very happy, stable marriage. So powerful is the gift of listening that it can help you build and maintain one of the most satisfying marriages imaginable. Couples that do not learn this skill will have a very tough time of it, and their satisfaction in the marriage will likely diminish markedly over time.

Enough said about how important listening is. Let's move on to how to develop the art of listening in a marriage.

If partners want to develop the art of listening, they must practice it and follow a few rules as they do. The rules are simple, but they must be adhered to for successful and satisfying communication to take place.

The Rules of Listening

If you are the person listening, you must:

1. Agree to a time to listen and stop what you are doing during this time

2. Maintain eye contact with your spouse

3. Ask non-judgmental questions

4. Clarify what is being said and ask if it is accurate

5. Re-clarify if necessary

6. Refrain from expressing your own thoughts and feelings

7. Refrain from offering solutions

8. Refrain from blaming

9. Refrain from offering advice

10. Refrain from getting defensive

If you are the person talking, you must:

1. Request that your spouse take some time to listen to you

2. State your views as completely as possible

3. State your feelings

4. Refrain from blaming

5. Refrain from criticism, sarcasm and put-downs

The person who is doing the listening has the lion's share of the responsibility. However, in order for the discussion to come off successfully both parties must adhere to their set of rules. Once the person doing the talking agrees that he or she has been fully understood, the person doing the listening can request that his or her views be heard. In this case, the partners switch roles and the process begins again.

While much training can be done on the particulars of listening like how to clarify and how to ask non-judgmental questions, I don't think most people need it. Knowing how to clarify and ask questions is not the problem. The problem lies in keeping emotions in check and refraining from breaking rules six through ten. This takes practice and self-control. To become good at it takes years. During that time patience must be exercised on both sides.

It should be pointed out, too, that the person talking must also become practiced at bridling the expressions of his or her emotions. While on the one hand it is perfectly okay to express how you feel, you must learn to stop short of blaming the other person for how you feel. One way of doing this is by using ABC statements. In ABC statements you use this format: "When you do A in situation B, I feel C." In reality it might go something like, "When you sit and watch television when I am cleaning house, I feel angry." Or, "When you give me the silent treatment when I don't agree with you about something, I get angry and frustrated."

By using such a format, blame, criticism, sarcasm and put-downs are avoided. It also provides a format for making your message clear.

It is still possible for the listener to feel blame despite the ABC format, even when there is no intention of assigning blame. This is where self-control comes in. Even if blame is what is being felt the listener must refrain from expressing it. Rather, he or she must stick to the role of listener and clarify what is being said and felt. The best way of doing this is to simply "mirror" back what the other person has said. For example, "What I hear you saying is that when I sit and watch television while you clean the house, you get angry. Is that right?" Or, "What I hear you saying is that when I give you the silent treatment when you disagree with me, you get angry and frustrated. Is that right?" If it isn't quite right, then the person doing the talking should re-express his or her thoughts and feelings and the listener should clarify them once again.

All of this takes patience and practice. But, wow, is it worth it! If you can master the art of listening, your chance for a satisfying marriage dramatically increases. Remember, though, that there will still likely be times when emotions override your spouse's ability to practice the rules of listening.

Love Potion #11

Pick out something you would like to discuss. Choose something that is not too emotionally charged. You may even like to choose something that has no emotional charge to it whatsoever, such as something happening in the news. Take turns being the listener and the talker. First practice following the rules of listening as stated in this chapter. Then discuss the rules you could have broken and how this would have affected the conversation. Take a break and have a wrestling match. Tickling is encouraged!

The Art of Settling Arguments: Part Two

As I pointed out in the last chapter, arguments often dissipate without anyone ever having to do anything other than listen to and understand the other's point of view. The process can almost seem magical. Each and every time this process is successfully completed, the love bond between the partners is strengthened.

However, there are other times when just listening and understanding is not enough. Decisions must be made and actions carried out. How to do this in a way that preserves and strengthens the marriage is the subject of this chapter.

Some people fear that by bringing up areas of conflict they are putting their marriage at risk. This isn't the case. Couples that learn to deal with discord successfully are the ones likely to stay happily married. Avoiding conflict leads to problems. The longer negative feelings and thoughts are repressed, the stronger they become. Then they are likely to either come out sideways or with such emotion that it is difficult for either person to deal with them rationally. It is far better to deal with differences as they come up than to put them off to fester.

So let me suggest a problem-solving formula. If you follow it, you will be able to solve virtually any problem that comes your way as a couple. However, it is absolutely essential to preface this process with both partners expressing their views and feelings until they feel like the other understands fully. Keep in mind that I am not saying there must be agreement; rather, there should be understanding. Once mutual understanding has been reached, employing the problem-solving strategy will be easy and highly effective.

The Problem-Solving Strategy

The first step in employing the problem-solving strategy is to agree what the problem is to be solved. To answer this question it is necessary first to lay aside any feelings of blame. This should be fairly easy to do if you have already made the effort to listen to and understand each other's point of view.

Some problems are small and easy to identify. Others are more complex and have numerous elements to them. For example, deciding where to go out to eat is one thing, solving financial problems another. (However, I must admit that for some couples, coming to agreement on a place to eat can be a major problem.) If the problem is a more complex one, it is advisable to break it down into smaller parts you can deal with one at a time. By breaking problems down, couples can avoid becoming overwhelmed.

One example of this might be dealing with financial problems. This is a good example, as financial problems have many facets to them and are also highly emotionally charged. After discussing the problem using the rules of listening, the couple would break it down into smaller parts, something like credit card management, ways to spend less, ways to bring in more money, bill-paying and checkbook-management. Once the problem is broken down, tackle the smaller, easier elements first; once those are solved, work on the more difficult ones.

Once you have agreed what the problem is to be worked on, you are ready to go on to the next step, which is to brainstorm solutions. While the process of brainstorming is a fairly simple one, NASA developed some guidelines that work extremely well and are used in businesses from Microsoft to Disney. Couples can put them to use just as effectively as businesses. The rules are as follows.

The Rules of Brainstorming

1. The ideas should be written down

2. Any idea can be suggested

3. No idea should be evaluated during the process, verbally or non-verbally (in other words, no making faces!)

4. Be creative (silly ideas can have wonderful potential for opening the door to great ideas)

5. Stick with it when you get stuck. Use some humor to get it going again.

This process should be a fun one, and it has the potential to provide solutions you may have otherwise missed. It can also relieve tension and give a couple a sense of hope and teamwork.

Step three in the problem-solving strategy is to agree on a specific solution that you both would be willing to try out. This may take some compromise. It may also take putting two or three ideas from your brainstorming session together. To facilitate the process of deciding, go back over the ideas from the brainstorming session and mark all ideas that appeal to either of you. Then go back and identify any ideas that both of you like and can agree upon.

If there is no obvious agreement between the two of you, pick an idea that you would both be willing to try for a set period of time, after which you will come back and assess the results. The key to this step is agreeing on a specific solution with specific actions clearly assigned and agreed upon. And these agreements must be made in a way that both people's needs are focused on rather than just one person's (please see the first chapter on Harmony Theory).

Step four is to follow up, if it's a solution that will be enacted over time. Some problems are short in duration and once a solution is agreed upon and put into place there is no need for further discussion; an example of this might be deciding where to go on vacation. Other problems need long-term solutions, like financial problems.

If the problem you are solving is long-term in nature, decide when you will come back to assess it. When you do return to the discussion, talk about whether or not the idea is working. If it is, discuss whether there are any ways to improve on it. If the solution isn't working, go back to the third step and pick another solution you're both willing to give a whirl. If you can't find one, hold another brain-storming session.

At every step in this process it is critical to respect each other's ideas and feelings. Blame and anger must be checked and left out if the problem-solving strategy is to produce results.

Every bit of time and effort a couple puts into learning and employing the problem-solving process is worthwhile. Each and every time it is successfully completed your love will grow and your marriage will strengthen.

Love Potion #12

Set aside some time to practice the problem-solving strategy. Pick a problem that you would like to solve but start out with something that isn't highly emotionally charged. In other words, in the beginning stay away from issues that always seem to lead to angry or hurt feelings. Have some fun with it. Get out some snacks and put on your favorite music. Plan to make love when you get done.

How to Get Your Point Across Without Using Criticism

The most corrosive thing you can do in a love relationship is to frequently criticize your spouse. I say frequently because infrequent criticism probably won't sink a relationship. A steady diet of it, though, will damage a love relationship beyond repair.

When I talk about this in my seminars, people want to know how they're supposed to let someone know they're displeased without coming across as being critical. This is a good question, because for a happy marriage to exist the partners must be able to negotiate change. If this possibility does not exist, the marriage will either end emotionally or in the divorce courts.

A couple of ways of resolving conflict and negotiating change have already been suggested in other chapters. In this chapter we will deal with a slightly different strategy for negotiating change. I call it "Constructive Complaining."

There are three guidelines for making a complaint constructive. The first of these is to make the complaint specific. It cannot be global in nature or make use of a definitive. For example, it is okay to say something like, "I dislike it when you come home late without calling me." It is not okay to say, "You're always late and you never call me."

Second, in a constructive complaint you tell your spouse how you feel. Most often you can distill your feelings down into one or two words. Something like the following will work: "When you stay on the Internet all night, I feel lonely and unappreciated."

Third, constructive complaints are short. No more than a sentence or two is allowed. Following this guideline will help you stay away from blame, which has no place in a constructive complaint.

In a constructive complaint you can also follow the ABC format I describe in the chapter, "The Art of Settling Arguments: Part Two." To recap this format, you plug your feelings and thoughts into the following formula: "When you do A in situation B, I feel C." It would come out something like this: "When you don't get the things at the grocery store that I put on the list, I feel angry."

A constructive complaint is very different from a criticism. Criticism usually assigns blame and is less than specific. When people use criticism they also tend to go on and on. Criticism is emotionally charged and often leads to a fight. Rarely does criticism lead to a successful resolution; rather, it often leads to hurt feelings and thoughts of revenge.

Worse even than criticism is criticism capped with contempt. Contempt is found in statements that add insult to the criticism. In statements like these, the person may say something like, "Look at our house. You're such a slob." Or, statements like, "You'd spend half the weekend in bed if I let you. I've never met someone as lazy as you. No wonder we have financial problems."

Research of marital communication has established that couples who criticize or express contempt will likely divorce within three years. This is alarming if criticism is part of the way you communicate with your spouse. The good news is that it is possible to jettison the criticism in favor of constructive complaints. To do so takes a commitment, some self-control and lots of practice.

Let me end the subject of criticism with this analogy. When I went to the dentist to have my semi-annual cleaning, the hygienist asked me that question that every dental hygienist asks when he or she gets done cleaning your teeth—"Do you floss?"—to which I answered sheepishly, "Well, most of the time, but perhaps not as much as I should." She replied, "Well, you only need to floss if you want to keep your teeth." The same applies here—you only need to get rid of criticism if you want to keep your marriage together!

Love Potion #13

The next time you want to complain about something, stop yourself. Instead, take some time to write your complaint out. Follow
the guidelines for making a complaint constructive. Tell your spouse
that you have a constructive complaint and ask him or her to listen
to it and "mirror" it back to you before he or she responds to it. In
other words, your spouse is to say something like, "What I hear you
saying is that when I leave my clothes on the floor you get angry. Is
that right?"

Once he or she "mirrors" the complaint back, express your appreciation for hearing you correctly. Then ask if it would be okay to sched-
ule a brainstorming session to help resolve the problem (see the
chapter "The Art of Settling Arguments: Part Two"). Reward yourself
for doing such a good job by either going out for ice cream or gourmet coffee.

Do You Have the Self-Control and Emotional Maturity Necessary to Handle Conflict?

This chapter contains a test, a self-test to see if you have what it takes to handle conflict in your relationship in a healthy way. Actually, everyone does have the capacity to handle conflict well, but many do not yet know how to access or develop their skills. The first step in changing anything about you or your love relationship is figuring out what needs to be changed. This test is designed to help you reach some insight into what you might want to work on to handle conflict better.

The Conflict Readiness Test

Instructions: Answer the following questions true or false. Put a "T" for true and an "F" for false. Answer the questions as truthfully as possible. You do not need to show your answers to anyone. You may want to record your answers on a separate sheet of paper to maintain your privacy.

_____ 1. I would rather avoid conflicts

_____ 2. When my spouse complains to me, I often complain to him/her about something

_____ 3. I admit that I can be a bit sarcastic at times

_____ 4. I don't mean to, but once in a while I make a remark that is insulting to my spouse

_____ 5. Sometimes my spouse complains that I make too many excuses

_____ 6. Everyone knows I have a bad temper

_____ 7. When my spouse gets on my case, I leave the house

_____ 8. Once in a while I get my way by putting my spouse on a guilt trip

_____ 9. Sometimes I find myself thinking about how I can get back at my spouse

_____ 10. I try to control myself but sometimes I hit something when I get angry

_____ 11. I'm pretty good at using put-down humor

_____ 12. For me, keeping the peace is the best way to go about things

_____ 13. Don't tell anyone, but I use a few recreational drugs to relieve my stress

_____ 14. I've been known to make a few threats in order to get people to come around to my way of thinking

_____ 15. Sometimes I get so frustrated when I am arguing that I bring up all kinds of issues during the same argument

_____ 16. So often, I find that when other people give me negative feedback, they are way off-base

_____ 17. If you ever heard me arguing with my spouse you would hear me shoveling it all back in his/her direction

_____ 18. I drink to relax. I drink more when my spouse and I are fighting

_____ 19. I do my fair share of blaming

_____ 20. If you talked to my spouse, he/she would tell you I whine a lot

_____ 21. The more my spouse confronts me, the more I clam up

_____ 22. I hate it, but I tend to pout when I don't get my way

_____ 23. Sometimes my spouse puts me in a position that forces me to lie in order to keep the peace

_____ 24. Anybody would have trouble resolving conflict with my spouse

_____ 25. I complain too much

_____ 26. If you could look up the cliché about the pot calling the kettle black you would see a picture of my spouse

_____ 27. I know exactly what buttons to push to drive my spouse crazy. I know I shouldn't but sometimes I push them to get him/her to give in to me

_____ 28. I sleep a lot when things aren't going well at our house.

_____ 29. It's a good thing I have my friends and family to turn to when we are fighting

_____ 30. For anything my spouse can say about me, I have a retort

Now go back and change any answers you weren't totally truthful about. Then stop and think about how you felt when you were answering the questions. Was it a proud feeling? In other words, did you have the feeling you must be pretty good at resolving conflict? Or did you squirm a bit when you answered the questions? Did you think that the best thing to do was to destroy your answer sheet so no one would see it? If you showed your spouse your answers, which answers would he/she disagree with?

Scoring instructions: this self-test is also self-assessed. You either pass or fail according to the grade you give yourself. Please realize, though, that this instrument is meant to give you some insights into ways that you might change how you deal with conflict.

Love Potion #14

Take a risk and have your spouse take this test and answer the questions about you from his or her perspective. Rarely do we get an honest look at ourselves, so this is a good opportunity to get some feedback. Ask him or her to be as honest as possible and to give you the scoring sheet when finished. Vow not to become defensive and ask your spouse to explain his or her answers. Now kiss your spouse and say thank you.

Nine Ways Successful Couples Express Their Love Daily

Dr. John Gottman, professor of psychology at the University of Washington, studied over 2,000 couples and reported the results in his book, *Why Marriages Succeed or Fail.*

One thing he found was that stable couples had at least five times more positive interactions than negative ones—a 5 to 1 ratio. I think it is a safe assumption that the greater this ratio was, the better the marriage.

He also found that couples used a variety of ways to interact on a positive basis. Here are the nine categories of positive interaction Dr. Gottman reported.

Show Interest

One way a person can show love to a partner is by showing an active interest in his or her activities. This is done chiefly by taking the time to ask questions about the other's day. It is also important here to stop doing whatever you're doing while you ask the questions, and to ask appropriate follow-up questions like, "And then what happened?" A positive attitude that reflects a sincere interest is essential.

Express Affection

Obvious expressions of love (in ample quantities) like sexual inter-course, hugs, kisses, and verbal expressions are necessary in marriage. There are also smaller expressions of affection that are meaningful in a good love relationship. These can include things like holding hands, curling up on the couch together, spooning and playing "footsie" together. Many such little ways of expressing your affection can add up to a satisfying relationship.

Express Consideration

During major holidays, couples are normally fairly good at showing they care. Very happily married couples are also good at expressing how much they care on a daily basis. These expressions come normally through small actions that show consideration. These can include things like calling to say hi when you know your spouse has a tough day ahead, doing one of the household chores that he or she normally does, stopping to buy your spouse's favorite treat or doing something your spouse loves to do even though you'd rather be doing something else. Rarely do partners in happy, long-standing marriages point to the big things their spouses did for them over the years. Rather, they have loving recollections of the pattern of small acts of love.

Show Appreciation

One of the biggest reasons people choose the mate they do is because of the way they feel when they're with that person. And one of the ways people feel when they're feeling loved is appreciated. The expression of appreciation not only makes a person feel loved but it also increases the likelihood of expanding the very thing that is being appreciated. In other words, the more you appreciate someone for doing something, the more this person will want to continue doing that thing.

Unfortunately, in too many marriages the chief complaint is that the individuals feel unappreciated and taken for granted. Taking another person's efforts for granted is a very easy thing to do. But in happy marriages, both partners take action daily to make sure this does not happen. Rather, they go out of their way to let the other know that they are appreciated.

The things being appreciated can range from the large to the small: from expressing appreciation for working to support the family to helping with the dishes; from taking care of the children to the giving of a hug. The rule to keep in mind is that the more you express appreciation, the more you strengthen the love bond. Keep in mind too that expressing appreciation for small things counts more than the expected appreciation for the larger things.

Say You're Sorry

Regardless of the title of the movie to the contrary, love does mean having to say you're sorry. In love relationships, things are said and done that hurt. Many of these things are not intended to hurt, but they do nevertheless.

Loving people often know when they've said or done something to hurt their mate. Sometimes they know it a fraction of a second after they've made an insensitive remark. Once said, it is too late to take it back-but not too late to say you're sorry.

Saying you're sorry is tough for a lot of people. Why this is, I'm not sure. If it's easy for you, then you most likely do so whenever needed. If it's hard for you, then you'll have to find the courage. The good thing is that when you do, most spouses are extremely appreciative. Saying you're sorry for something may be just the start of making amends, but it's a good start.

Express Empathy

One kind of empathy can be expressed by listening to your partner's trials and tribulations and expressing your understanding and concern. This is a good thing to do on a regular basis.

Another kind of empathy puts yourself in your spouse's shoes. To do this, you must, of course, be sincere in your desire to express your compassion. Show that you truly want to know what it is like to be in your spouse's place at the moment. Ask as many questions as possible to get a complete picture of what is being experienced and the resulting feelings. When you think you have enough information, express to your spouse the respect you have for his or her struggles. Clarify how you think it must feel to go through what your spouse has and is going through.

This is a wonderful gift to give someone you love dearly. Not everyone can do it, but it is well worth the effort if you can.

Show Acceptance and Understanding

Sometimes it is a great relief in life to have someone who simply accepts the way you are. Especially if this person can take what you say and do without hassling you about it. All of these things come under the heading of unconditional love.

I don't think it is possible for a couple to show unconditional love for each other all of the time or even most of the time. But it is a wonderful feeling to have this unconditional love even for short periods of time. Sometime, when you know your spouse really needs it, or at a time when nothing particular is going on, tell your spouse how much you love him or her, that he or she doesn't need to change a thing in order for you to love them and that you foresee your love lasting through all eternity. Do this over a romantic dinner or when you are eating breakfast one morning.

Be Playful

Couples sometimes wonder if their teasing and silliness is normal or if one day they need to grow up. The truth of the matter is that we all have an inner child that wants to come out and play. For most people, the only safe place for this child to come and play is with their spouse. Playing around, teasing, sharing personal jokes and having an uproarious time together is not only okay but it will strengthen your love bond. The only caution is that the fun you are expressing must be fun to both partners. If not, then that particular expression of playfulness should be left out.

Share Laughter and Delight

There are many things to both laugh at and be delighted with in a day's time. Loving couples look for these things and they share them with their spouses. The more you can access your sense of humor and share your joy with your spouse the easier life and love will come.

Love Potion #15

In other chapters I talk about ways to successfully resolve conflicts. When it comes down to it, the very best way to resolve a conflict is to not have the conflict in the first place. And the best way I know to reduce the number of conflicts a couple has is for each of the partners to feel full of love. When a person feels filled with love, potential conflicts seem to melt away. So, the suggestion here is to express your love to your mate at least five times a day. Use as many of the different kinds of love expressions as you can. Here's my guarantee: Expressing your love five times a day will keep the divorce lawyers away!

What Every Person Needs for Love to Flourish

Love is a fascinating subject. To one degree or another, it interests almost everyone. It is not surprising, then, that scientists and researchers have put a lot of effort into studying the subject.

One of the things that researchers have clearly established about love relationships is that there is a direct correlation between the feelings of love a person has for someone else and how important and worthwhile the same person feels in the eyes of his or her mate. Put another way, the more appreciation you give your spouse, the more he or she will reciprocate with expressions of love.

This makes a lot of sense when you think about it. It is a great human need to feel valuable, to feel needed and appreciated. (This is evident at work, as well; when employees are asked what their employer can do to improve the workplace, one of the most common answers is to show more appreciation.) I think appreciation is so important because our sense of self-worth is very much related to the feedback we get from other people. If you read books on self-esteem, they will tell you that you should not rely on other people for your self-worth. But the fact is we do. Think about yourself for a moment. Do you not have a need to feel important in the eyes of those around you? Next, ask yourself how you know whether or not the people around you value you. One of the answers has to be through the expression of appreciation.

One thing is clear. People need to be recognized and appreciated for their positive qualities and contributions. If in a love relationship, they will reciprocate by expressing their love back. This process makes appreciation a true elixir of love.

You probably already know this is true. Yet I think we need to be reminded of it over and over again. Everyday life can take its toll; we get so busy and so wrapped up in doing all that we have to do that we don't get around to expressing appreciation to those we love.

Not taking the time to express appreciation to your mate can be deadly to the relationship. It's like neglecting to water and fertilize your plants. If you don't do it, they will wither and die. So will love. And just like plants, love needs to be nourished on a regular basis (daily is best).

So, what are the best ways to let the person you love know he or she is important to you and appreciated by you? There are two. One is to simply say "thank you." I don't think you can say thank you enough in a marriage. Never have I had someone in my office complain that his or her spouse says thank you too often. And it's important to say thank you for the small things, the mundane tasks that are done over and over again on a daily basis.

Another is to compliment. Expressing your admiration for a person's personal qualities goes a long way toward making someone feel loved. Complimenting how well someone does a particular thing is also valuable in building and maintaining a love relationship.

Three things will happen when you take the time and effort to express appreciation to the person you love. First, that person's love for you will grow. Second, your love for that person will grow. Third, the behaviors and qualities you focus on will increase. These should provide you with ample motivation to make sure you express at least some form of appreciation on a daily basis.

Love Potion #16

Here is a list of the top twenty-five behaviors that married couples engage in together. Each of these things can be both appreciated and complimented. Check the ones that you would like to see more of in your marriage. Start focusing on these areas and saying "thank you" for any and all things your partner does in these areas. At the same time look for any little things that you can compliment. Commit yourself to doing this for one month. At the end of the month go back over the list and see what has improved in your marriage. Express some appreciation and compliment your spouse on these improvements.

Here is the list. Remember to check the ones you want to expand. Then go back and circle the three most important ones. Focus most of your attention on appreciating and giving compliments in these areas.

Areas of Behavior

___ Affection

___ Arguing Skills

___ Attitude

___ Keeping Commitments

___ Communication Skills

___ Showing Consideration

___ Talking Things Over

___ Creativity

___ Handling Financial Matters

___ Flexibility

___ Friendship

___ Generosity

___ Gift-giving

___ Honesty

___ Household Tasks

___ Child Rearing

___ Giving Compliments

___ Listening Attentively

___ Lovemaking

___ Being Patient

___ Playfulness

___ Planning Romantic Activities

___ Sense of Humor

___ Sensitivity

___ Expressions of Appreciation

Mind Reading 101 or,— 'If You Loved Me, You Would Know'

Marital therapists warn of mind-reading. Typical mind-reading thoughts like, "If he loved me, he would have known what I wanted" or "If he doesn't know why I'm mad, I'm not going to tell him!," are said to be detrimental to a relationship. When they say this, they're really talking about two things. First, when you take action based on what you believe your spouse is thinking, you always run the risk of being wrong. And second, if you get angry when your spouse does not read your mind and do what you want, then you're likely to be angry a lot. This is the "bad" kind of mind-reading. But, there is a good kind of mind-reading too.

Happy couples, in fact, do it on a daily basis. They tend to know their spouses so well that they anticipate their spouses' needs and desires and take action to respond to them. For example, one partner knows that the other has had a really hard day, so he or she arranges to have a relaxing evening planned. Another time, one spouse may say no to an invitation, knowing the other would likely not want to go.

In happy marriages, such mind-reading is common. Even if the mind-reading is off-base, it doesn't do any harm. The person coming home from the hard day may well say, "Yes, it has been a hard day, but you know what? I think I'd love to go out dancing tonight." Or, "Actually I would like to accept that invitation. Would you mind if I called back and accepted it?"

Also, partners in successful relationships tend to be sensitive to each other's moods. Subtle non-verbal cues give them the ability to know when something is wrong. Often these cues will prompt questions like, "You seem preoccupied today. Would you like to talk about what's on your mind?" Or, "You aren't yourself today. What's going on with you?" Such questions are of great comfort to the person being asked; they make him or her feel loved and cared for on a very deep level.

In marriages in which mind-reading is a problem, partners are frequently incorrect and then base their actions on those false assumptions. Or, partners develop a pattern of interpreting each other's thoughts in a negative light. If this is the case in your relationship, these patterns must be broken. The way to do this is to make a commitment to each other to check before decisions are made and actions taken.

Make a habit of asking questions like, "You seem like you're angry with me. Is that right?" and "It seems to me that you would rather not go to that party. Is that right?" Using questions like these can dramatically improve the way a couple communicates. Not only do they clear up communication but also the mere asking of the questions communicates that you care about your spouse.

Love Potion #17

Practice mind-reading with your spouse. Agree to make a game of it for a few weeks. Here are the rules. At least once a day read each other's minds and determine how you think your spouse is feeling or what he or she is thinking. Then check it out with questions like, "What I think you are thinking right now is that we should not go out tonight. Is that right?" Or, "What I think you are feeling right now is disappointment. Is that right?" Keep score and decide what the winner gets when the two weeks are up.

The Most Important Investment You Can Make

Time. That's the most important investment you can make in your marriage. Consider this: the average American finds time to watch between two and three hours of television a day but typically spends an average of eighteen minutes a week of quality time with a spouse.

Quality time is defined as time spent together talking attentively, expressing physical affection, discussing things only related to the two of you (parenting issues don't count), looking at each other, having fun, relaxing (television time doesn't count, as it does nothing positive for the relationship), eating quietly, and spending time worshiping or praying. Accounting for all of the above, the average length of quality time spent in a marriage was eighteen minutes a week. This research was conducted by Dr. Paul Pearsall with over 5,000 couples and reported in his book, *Super Marital Sex*.

Eighteen minutes a week. That's not much, is it? In fact, I don't know much that you can do for only eighteen minutes a week that will produce a lot of good results. When you think about it, all the other major activities of our life like work, taking care of the household and children all take up hours and hours. We even spend more time doing the laundry and cutting the grass. Yet one of the most important aspects of our life is our marriage and we typically spend less than an hour a week really "with" our spouse.

Perhaps you're thinking that this may be true for other people but certainly not for you. If so, I invite you to take the following test. It is similar to the one that was given to the couples in Dr. Pearsall's research.

The Quality Marital Time Test

Instructions: Estimate the average amount of minutes you spend each week in the following activities.

1. _____ minutes
   Time spent looking at each other only to admire the other person

2. _____ minutes
   Time spent talking about your marriage

3. _____ minutes
   Time spent discussing the news

4. _____ minutes
   Time spent just being together while one person does something like read, sew or listen to music. Television time does not count, as it is more like hypnosis than quality time.

5. _____ minutes
   Time spent eating alone together

6. _____ minutes
   Time spent worshiping, meditating or praying together.

7. _____ minutes
   Time spent talking with your spouse about things that only concern the two of you. Do not count time discussing children or in-laws. Also, only count time spent talking with the television off.

8. _____ minutes
   Time spent hugging, making love, kissing and touching. Do not count quick hugs and kisses or touching while sleeping

9. _____ minutes
   Time spent walking leisurely together. Do not count speed walking.

   _____ minutes
   Total Quality Marital Minutes

In the research that was conducted, participants not only could not count time watching television, but also had to subtract any time spent watching television from the total quality minutes. The reason given for this was because Dr. Pearsall views television to be an addiction that robs the couple of valuable time that could be spent on intimacy. I leave it up to you to decide whether this is a valid point in your marriage.

Getting back to the test, how do you feel about the results? Are you happy with the amount of quality time you're spending together? Or are you thinking it would be a good idea to increase the amount of quality time you spend with your spouse?

Love Potion #18

Go out to breakfast or lunch on the weekend, together and alone. Take a pad and pencil and the Quality Marital Time Test with you. Have each of you pick the number one area in which you would like to spend more quality time together. Spend ten minutes on each area brainstorming ways you can increase the time spent. Pick one or two ideas from each list and make a commitment to put them into action next week.

Establishing Priorities (Preferably the Right Ones)

Whether or not a couple takes the time to talk about and set their priorities, the priorities get set anyway. As married life progresses, choices are made and more time gets allotted to some things than others.

In America, if you ask people to list their priorities in rank order, most will say the same thing. They will list them as:

1. God

2. Family

3. Work

4. Recreation

While this list is common, it is curious for two reasons. First, it doesn't specifically include the marriage. Second, it is rarely the way many people order their lives in reality.

While I don't want to suggest to couples what priorities are right to adopt, I would like to stress that the marriage should be near the top of the list.

Marriage should come before all other people, events and activities. Even before the children. In fact, the best thing you can do for your children is to put your marriage first. The better the relationship between you and your spouse, the better you will be able to attend to the needs of your children. Even work benefits from a happy marriage. People who are happily married are healthier and miss less work.

Love Potion #19

Write a love letter to your spouse. In it, say how much you enjoy being with him or her—that he is your top priority, why she is so important to you. List the qualities you admire in him. Get a love stamp and mail the card or put it in her pillowcase so she will find it at bedtime.

Forgiveness for Heartbreak and Pain

Forgiveness is an easy concept. We are told from the time we're children that we're supposed to both apologize if we do something that hurts someone else and forgive if someone does something to harm us. Parents teach forgiveness, as does every major religion. You would think that with all of this teaching it would be easy to forgive. But it's not.

A lot of variables go into our decision to forgive. It depends on things like:

1. The degree of hurt we feel

2. Whether we assess the act to be premeditated or an accident

3. How many times the person has done the same or similar things

4. How much we love the person

5. How much we depend on the person

6. Our mood at the time

7. How loved we are feeling at the time

8. The behaviors surrounding forgiving that we observed in our parents

9. The degree to which our religion influences us

10. Whether or not we are willing to continue putting energy into holding a grudge

11. Whether or not the person committing the offense is contrite

12. What we are watching on television or reading in a book at the moment

13. The advice we get from family and friends

14. How stressed we are at the moment

15. How many times the person has forgiven us

With all of these variables affecting our decision to forgive or not, it is no wonder that forgiveness does not come easily. But it must, if love is to survive and flourish. Love relationships are dependent on forgiveness. In love mistakes are made, some on purpose and some by accident or sins of omission. There is no way around it. This being the case, every partner in every love relationship must learn to give and receive forgiveness.

When it comes down to it, love cannot blossom if either person in the relationship is full of anger, rage or resentment. Rather, love must confront errors, mistakes, faults, omissions and hurts—and forgive them all.

Forgiveness is not an option in a marriage. Either it is present in the measure necessary for the survival of that marriage or the marriage will end either emotionally or in the divorce courts.

What this all means is that forgiveness is serious business. The couples that have the happiest marriages over a period of time learn to forgive and forget. Other couples forgive but don't forget. These can still be happy, stable marriages. In some of the couples that have more trouble, the partners want forgiveness for themselves but are unwilling to give it. In other troubled couples, the partners hold and feed their grudges.

The goal, then, for those couples wishing to build and maintain a happy marriage is to learn to forgive and forget. If they cannot forget, the partners must learn to at least forgive. While forgiveness is not always easy, it is possible. Love Potion #22 provides a doorway into forgiveness if you are having trouble doing so.

Love Potion #20

Set aside some time—about an hour—to write a letter to your spouse. The letter you are going to write is for your eyes only. It is not to be shared with your spouse or anyone else.

Pick an issue that you are upset with your spouse about. Start writing everything you think and feel. Don't worry about being reasonable, rational or logical. Just write whatever comes to mind. Include all of your fears and suspicions.

State in the letter how you wish your spouse would act toward you and how you think he or she should handle the problem at hand. Make sure to write about how you feel—any hurt, shame, betrayal, jealousy, blame, sadness, anger, fear and resentment. Write about anything you might do to get your spouse back for hurting you.

Once you are satisfied that you have committed all of your negative thoughts and feelings to paper, start a second letter. In this letter, write about the love and compassion that you feel for your spouse. Talk about understanding how he or she could have messed up and that you forgive him or her. Write about your spouse's good points and how much you appreciate him or her. If you have any trouble writing the positive letter, think of the kindest, most forgiving person you know and imagine that this person is helping you write the letter.

When you're done writing both letters, burn the first letter (safely, please). Then decide whether or not you want to give your spouse the second letter. If not now, save it in a safe place to give at a later time. Now go treat yourself to something you love to eat or do.

The Myth that Can Torpedo Your Marriage

There are a lot of myths about marriage, but there is one very common myth that is so destructive it can cause the break-up of the marriage. The myth is this: If that wonderful, passionate feeling you had when you married goes away, the love must have gone out of the marriage. This is often expressed between spouses when one says to the other, "I love you, but I'm not 'in love' with you anymore."

What's really being expressed is a belief that the couple should always have that loving feeling the marriage started out with. And who can blame them? It is wonderful to experience the heightened passion of falling in love.

But the myth is dangerous to marriages because of the behavior that can result from it. What happens so often is this: when one of the partners concludes that love has flown the coop, he or she is ripe for someone else to come along and fill the void. Very quickly, a new love relationship can form. Then, the passion of a new relationship convinces the person that true love has been found at last. He or she rushes to end the present marriage and marry the "true love."

I wish it were a requirement of marriage that everyone sign a disclaimer accepting that real love starts where passionate love leaves off. Then I wish a post card reminding the couple of this fact be mailed to them every month for two years, starting the thirteenth month of the marriage. This would help get most through the turbulent time when the honeymoon ends, the love blinders come off and passionate love flies the coop.

Since this is unlikely to happen, please feel free to copy this chapter and give it to the newlyweds you know. Better yet, buy the book for them and put a note in it suggesting they read this chapter first.

Remember, the marriage you save may produce the parents of your future grandchildren!

Love Potion #21

Go to bed a half an hour early tonight. Light some candles and put on your favorite music. Snuggle and recall what it was like when the two of you fell in love. Talk both of how you felt and of the things you did together. Recall for one another the reasons you wanted to marry the other person. Then let nature take its course.

Keeping Romance Alive and How to Rekindle It if It Wanes

It's too bad, but romance doesn't happen automatically. Romance takes a commitment and a determined effort by both partners. Even in the honeymoon period, a lot of effort goes into being romantic. It may seem to happen automatically, but in reality both people put themselves totally into the experience of being loving to each other. They do this, of course, because of how wonderful they feel in the presence of their lovers. So, while they're putting a lot of effort into the relationship, it doesn't feel that way because they want to so badly.

Putting this kind of effort into you marriage after the honeymoon stage ends results in a much bigger payoff—mature love. Mature love between people is just as wonderful as young love. It is a love that is full of compassion, kindness, appreciation, commitment, forgiveness and understanding. It even has its periods of extreme passion.

This kind of mature love is the stuff that enables being happily married for a lifetime. Because you are reading this book, I assume you're very interested in either keeping romance alive or rekindling it. If this is true, I highly recommend the following love potion to you.

Love Potion #22

Take out a sheet of paper and write out the sentence, "I feel loved when you..." Complete the sentence and then start over. Continue until you have a minimum of thirty-five answers. Write as fast as you can and complete the sentence with anything that comes to mind. Sometimes your best and most revealing answers will seem to come out of nowhere.

Now write out the sentence, "When we were first in love, I felt loved when you..." In the same fashion, quickly rewrite and complete the sentence at least fifteen times. Some of your answers may be repeats. That's okay.

Once you have this done, repeat the process with the sentence, "I would like you to show me love by..." Complete this sentence at least ten times. Use different answers than you did in the first two sentences.

Last, complete the sentence, "I feel romantic when..." at least ten times.

Now combine your lists, putting a number one by the items that are most important to you.

Exchange lists with your spouse. Vow to one another that you will do at least two things per day off of your partner's list. Make sure to express your appreciation when your partner does so, too.

The Biggest Shock in Marriage

In early love, we feel totally cared for when we're with our lover. The reason for this is simple. Our cherished one does everything possible to take care of our needs. He or she seems to have an uncanny ability to know just what we desire at any given moment and to fulfill that need. Not since we were young children under the protection of our mothers have we experienced that kind of total fulfillment and caring. It feels so good that we will do anything to keep this wonderful person in our lives (and fulfilling our every need).

Of course, the best way we know to keep this person in our lives is to ferret out his or her every need and to satisfy it. This in turn causes our loved one to feel deeply cared about, which reinforces his or her desire to keep fulfilling our needs. What a wonderful cycle! Too bad it has to end.

At some point in every relationship, one of the partners starts attending to his or her own needs more than to those of the mate's needs. This happens not by conscious design, but because of human nature. While it feels awesome to have someone attend so closely to our needs, there is no way that another person can know and satisfy all of them. To complicate things, at any given moment on any given day, our needs change. So, a different cycle in the relationship starts.

In this new cycle, one person has a need that is not being met, so he or she does whatever is necessary to satisfy this need. Sooner or later, the other person notices and is naturally left then to attend to his or her own needs. Which, of course, takes time and attention away from satisfying his or her partner's needs. Eventually each of the individuals spends more and more of time attending to individual needs.

What a shock this is. First you have someone attending to your every whim. Then, almost overnight, you find this person not only attending to his or her own needs, but also putting them above your needs.

In real life, it all happens something like this. During early love, the couple discusses plans for the weekend. The woman wants to go to the beach and suntan while the man is dying to go fishing with his friends. But he remembers the incredible back rub his darling fiancée gave him last night, so he lovingly says to her something like, "I can't think of anything I would rather do than take you to the beach." She smiles and replies, "You are so wonderful! All of your friends are going off fishing. Are you sure you wouldn't rather be with them?" To which he replies, "Not a chance. It's the weekend and I want to be with you, darling." She then says, "How very lucky I am to have a great guy like you. But tomorrow you are going fishing. I don't want to hear another word about it." Both then spend the weekend feeling totally at peace and completely cared for.

Fast-forward a couple of years, and the same scenario is played out in a dramatically different way. Let's say the couple is again making weekend plans. The wife says, "I would really like to go to the beach and tan on Saturday." The husband says, "I hate the beach. I'm going fishing, if you don't mind. I mean, you can go to the beach with your sister, can't you?" The wife replies, "Why can't we ever do something I want to do?" The husband's retort comes back, "It's the weekend. That's the only time I have to go fishing. Besides, we always do what you want. I never get to do what I want." This often ends up in a big fight with both partners feeling unloved and uncared for. These feelings in turn cause the partners to focus more intensely on making sure their own needs get met.

Tragically, when this happens, both the husband and wife are at great risk of falling in love with someone else. Somehow, somewhere they may well meet someone of the opposite sex and have an affair. During the affair, the early love cycle starts over again. Each of the people becomes intensely wrapped up in satisfying the other's needs and in so doing they fall deeply in love. And, knowing their husbands and wives are no longer attending to their needs, they divorce them in favor of this new person who does care enough about them to do so. I'll give you three guesses what happens next.

Couples that are able to stay together and build happy marriages figure out at some point that to be happy they must strike a balance between satisfying their own needs and satisfying the needs of their spouse. This is not an easy realization to come to. There is a part of us that will always believe that if our spouse truly loved us he or she would take care of us the way he or she used to. When we don't have evidence of this, it's natural to feel betrayed. If the couple is immature, this feeling of betrayal is hard to overcome and too often leads to divorce.

Even if a legal divorce does not take place, an invisible one often does. In an invisible divorce, partners find ways to avoid intimacy with each other. There are all kinds of mechanisms for this, including excessive drinking, spending time with friends, watching television, reading, spending time on the computer (especially in chat rooms), working out, shopping, fantasizing, going to bed early, staying up late, camping out on the phone, hobbies, volunteering, masturbating, complaining, refusing to make love, refusing to talk, going out drinking, going to the movies alone, having sex but not making love, falling asleep on the couch, coming home late, bringing work home from the office, taking drugs, reading every word of the newspaper and spending too much time with the children.

Please note that I said invisible divorces are made up of doing these things excessively. Most all of them in moderation are normal activities and are just fine. But taken to excess they are effective means of ending a marriage without ending it legally. These things allow the partners to completely avoid being intimate with each other. By intimacy, I don't mean sexual intimacy (though that can suffer greatly too). The kind of intimacy I am talking about is when two people share their lives together in harmony. A couple who is able to achieve this kind of intimacy can have an awesome marriage with both partners' needs being met.

But to get to this point, every couple must make it through the shock of finding out that their spouses aren't on this earth to satisfy their every need as their mothers once did. This is a formidable task. In fact, current statistics from the University of Wisconsin show that 67% of couples married after 1985 get divorced. The good news is that you can build and maintain the marriage of your dreams. How to do so is the subject of this book.

Suffice it to say, in this chapter, my goal is for couples to know about the shock they must overcome before they can go on to a long-term, satisfying relationship. As well, it is wise to take stock of the possible ways you might be avoiding intimacy with your spouse.

Love Potion #23

Go out for pizza, just the two of you. Get a booth and sit on the same side as lovers often do. Or, make "goo goo" eyes across the table while holding hands. Reminisce about the things you did together when you first fell in love. Ask each other about your favorite things to do together during that time (other than making love!). Make plans to do those things as soon as possible.

Advanced Forgiveness

One clear difference between couples that succeed and couples that fail is the ability to forgive. In great marriages, couples forgive and forget. In lousy marriages, the couples nurse grudges and plan revenge. There are many couples that lie somewhere in between these two extremes.

Where a couple falls on this continuum between forgiveness and vengeance depends a great deal on the age and maturity of the partners. It is unreasonable to expect young couples to "forgive and forget"; the best I think they can hope to achieve is to learn to forgive without forgetting. Only after years of marriage and lots of practice forgiving will a couple come to both forgive and forget.

One of the toughest hurdles young couples have to overcome is accepting that both partners are going to make mistakes. Some will be accidental, while others will result from poor judgment. And some will simply be selfish and thoughtless acts.

When you feel like your spouse has done something wrong on purpose, it's only natural to think, "If my spouse really loved me, he (or she) would not have done this to me." What is difficult for young couples to realize is that both partners, by virtue of being human, are only trying to satisfy their own needs. Most of what people do in life is not "to" someone but rather in an effort to satisfy a personal need. And even if the action is done "to" someone else, it is still carried out because of a perceived need. For example, revenge is motivated by a need (albeit dysfunctional) to respond to anger or hurt.

Knowing that all people are motivated primarily by their own needs helps us understand that our spouse's actions are most likely not intended to hurt us, but rather to satisfy a prevailing personal need.

Focusing on our partner's needs can help us empathize, or understand the reasons for those actions. And empathy helps us to forgive.

Still, as difficult as it is to forgive, we must have some motivation to do so. There are several such motivations. One is religious. Most religions teach us to forgive those who offend us. Another motivation is our own need for peace of mind. Since peace of mind and hate cannot coexist, we must either forgive or sacrifice at least a portion of our peace of mind. A third motivation comes from the knowledge that a stable and happy marriage cannot exist without forgiveness. Therefore, either learn to forgive or give up your chances for a happy marriage. Please realize, too, that you cannot avoid this issue by finding another spouse. If you find another spouse, learning forgiveness will still be a prerequisite to a happy marriage.

Love Potion #24

This is an advanced exercise in forgiveness. While it is highly worthwhile for couples to do the exercise together, it won't be easy. Do not do this exercise if either of you are tired, feeling irritable or are at odds with each other. Set a maximum time limit on this exercise of ninety minutes. If you don't finish, which is likely, you can set a date to come back to complete it on another day. Before you start, decide what you can reward yourselves with when you're done. Going out to eat or to a movie might be nice. What do you think?

Begin by both of you writing out two lists each. On your first list write down any things you're angry with your spouse about. Include things you're feeling resentful of. This first list represents the things you need to forgive your spouse for. (Hint: write them down even if you don't feel like you can or want to forgive these things right now).

On the second list write down things that you know you've done to anger or upset your spouse. Write only the things he or she is aware of—this is not meant to be an exercise in confessing. Make sure to include things that you don't feel you deserve to be forgiven for. This list represents the things you need to be forgiven for.

Once your lists are complete, flip a coin to see who goes first. Whoever wins the toss gets to choose. Then discuss one item from one of your first lists followed by one off the other's first list. Discuss each one thoroughly and then trade off, discussing an item from each of your second lists. As each of you listen to the other talk, abide by the rules of listening as stated in the chapter entitled, "The Art of Settling Arguments: Part One."

The purpose of this exercise is to clear the air of both resentment and guilt. For some couples the results can be cathartic. Now express your affection and go do the fun thing you planned to do before you started this very difficult exercise.

How to Establish Your Own Traditions
(to Form a Rock-Solid Marriage)

In early marriage, couples associate traditions with the ones that existed in their families. Quite naturally, each partner is attached to doing things the way they were done in his or her childhood. But in order for a marriage to thrive, partners must establish their own rituals.

In view of all the many traditions you grew up with, this may seem to be an almost insurmountable task. It isn't, though. What it takes is willingness on the parts of both partners to let go of the way their parents did things, even if it seems perfectly reasonable not to. Why? Because it's critical for couples to break their bonds with their parents. It is the first task of marriage (see the chapter entitled "The Essential Tasks of Marriage"). Before I go on, one caveat: religious traditions are important, and may be carried out in the manner dictated by your faith.

The good news is that it can be a lot of fun establishing your own traditions. It takes some creativity and some effort, but the work pays off in traditions that will endear you to each other, and that your children will come to look forward to. These new traditions will be what make your family unique.

So just what are traditions, anyway? Traditions are ways in which we come to celebrate life's significant events. In short, they are celebrations. Some traditions are big, some small. They can denote anything from the unique way we greet each other to the way we celebrate a major holiday or a birthday.

The smaller traditions most often "just happen." No one really plans them; rather, they evolve naturally. For example, my wife and I poke each other whenever one of us says something the other disagrees with. How this started is a mystery to me, but it provides us with a lot of laughs. We've also established a tradition over the years of coming home and spending ten minutes or so in our bedroom unwinding and talking about our day. Another is our rule for making the bed: the last one out has to do it. (We've had a lot of fun with this, but the winner often cheats and makes the bed while the loser is in the shower.) Simple and silly things like this are the glue that holds relationships together.

Here are some daily activities, along with some suggestions. Attach personal touches to make them unique.

Every Day Activities

1. **Going to bed**: spooning, saying something special, taking turns praying, reading out loud to each other

2. **Getting up**: taking turns selecting and playing music, a morning back scratch or massage or exercise together

3. Leaving in the morning: share plans for the day, predict positive results, remind each other of a positive trait each of you has, kiss passionately

4. **Connecting during the day**: meet for lunch on Tuesdays, send flowers, put love notes where each will find them throughout the day, call and listen to each other breathe, call to say I love you, e-mail a love note, pick out a sound and agree that every time you hear it you'll think loving thoughts about each other (such as bells ringing, a bird chirping, children playing or a door closing)

5. **Coming home**: establish a sanctuary where you can meet undisturbed for a few minutes to unwind and share the day's events, have a glass of wine or a soft drink together or go for a walk

6. **Suppertime**: have a pizza or hamburger night, have an eat-out night, have a TV tray night, have a night when one cooks the other's favorite meal, do the dishes together with your favorite music on loud or have one night a week when you eat fast food

7. **Evenings**: back rubs on Thursdays, go to bed an hour early on Wednesdays and read or do what comes naturally, watch your favorite television show together, take turns providing a special snack during your favorite show or have a board game night

8. **Weekends**: take turns planning something special to do on the weekends, take turns making breakfast for each other, do errands together and have brunch while you're out or try a different restaurant every weekend

There is no end to the variety of things you can turn into your own traditions. The same is true for the major holidays. The major holidays take more effort because of the emotional attachment people have to the traditions they grew up with. However, given time, patience and understanding these traditions can be tailor-made or adapted for your family, as well. One good way to start is by talking with each of your in-laws about how they started their traditions. In so doing, you will get great information, and you will likely feel a bit freer to establish your own way special ways to celebrate the holidays. After all, your parents did!

Love Potion #25

When you come home from work, ask each other to play the FNW game with you. In this game each partner completes the following sentences out loud: "I feel," "I need" and "I want." For example, "I feel tired," "I need to sit down and rest" and "I want to take the phone off the hook while I rest." Take turns completing the FNW sentences. Mirror the FNW sentences back to your mate: "What I hear you saying is that you feel tired, you would like to rest and you want the phone off the hook. Is that right?" Once in a while, for the fun of it, see if you can read each other's minds.

Taming the Money Monster: Part One

A couple's ability to handle financial matters is one of the variables that help determine the stability and happiness of the marriage. In great marriages, couples learn how to handle money matters together and to spend less than they make. The more trouble couples have doing this, the less stable and happy the marriage is.

This too is a task that takes time and effort to master. What that means is that for most couples it will take some time, even years, to sort out and master the money monster. During this time it helps to have some patience with each other, learning in the meantime as much as you can to help get your finances under control.

To start the process, it is enormously helpful in a marriage if the partners take the other's views on money. To help you do this, here are some sentence completions for each of you. This can be done verbally or the answers can be written down. If you wish, you can give several endings to each answer, but each answer should relate to money.

1. I think money is....

2. As a child, my family was....

3. I think you think money is....

4. When we fight about money I wish you would....

5. We disagree about money because....

6. We would get along better about money if I would....

7. When we fight about money I know you are only trying to....

8. We could have more money if....

9. My parents always told me....

10. I have had my worst problems with money when....

11. I have had my best success with money when...

12. If you really knew me you would know that...

13. We would not have any problems with money if....

14. What I know about financial matters I learned....

15. In the long run I think....

16. In the short term, I think we should....

17. The thing I like about the way we deal with money is....

18. My greatest fear about money is....

19. In order to improve our marriage I would be willing to....

20. I am optimistic about our financial situation because....

Once each of you has taken a turn answering these questions, take a walk and talk about what you learned from each other. Complete the following sentence during your discussion: "I was surprised to know...." Discuss what decisions you want to make in light of this information.

Love Potion #26

How long has it been since you went on a honeymoon? Plan an evening of soft music and candles. Talk about where you would like to go on a second honeymoon. Set a date to go. Follow up by getting travel brochures, finding out what the costs are and putting together a plan to finance it.

Taming the Money Monster: Part Two

In this chapter you will find the most commonly suggested steps for couples to take in order to gain control of their finances. It's not the easiest thing in the world to do, but it will be enormously helpful if both of you are willing to participate. Even couples with no financial problems may want to do it because of the potential insights that can be gained.

Money Monster Mania

There are three steps to Money Monster Mania. The first one takes a major commitment and is tough to do. The other two are a lot of fun. Put the three steps together and what you get is a whole lot more control over your finances. Plus, you will likely greatly improve your chances of being happily married for a lifetime!

Step One

Write down every cent you spend every day for a month. Every cent. No matter what you spend the money on, write it down. Also, save your receipts from everything and make notes on them so at the end of the month you'll be able to remember what the receipt was for.

This step is not so you can prepare a budget, though I suppose you could use the information for that purpose. Rather, you're doing this in order to give the two of you some knowledge and insight into your spending habits. Most couples have no idea where the extra money goes or in what quantities. For example, do you know how much you spent on eating out last month? How about on incidentals? If you already know the answers to these questions then you most likely already have the information this activity will yield. If not, then Money Monster Mania is for you.

Just thinking about writing down everything you spend will likely bring up some fears or other negative emotions. Talk with each other about your fears and any resistance you have to completing this activity.

When the month is up, take a sheet of legal paper and lay it on its side. Write across the top of the paper the different categories in which you spent your money. Use smaller categories than entertainment—break it down into movies, restaurants and movie rentals. If you are familiar with a computer spreadsheet program, you may want to enter the information into your computer. Enter in all of what you spent and total the columns.

Now discuss the results (please note: money issues are very touchy and can make people fearful and defensive. So, be kind and gentle with each other as you have your discussion). Ask yourselves these questions.

1. Which categories surprise or even shock you? Why?
2. Do you feel like you got your money's worth in each category?
3. In which categories do you think you overspent?
4. Which categories do you want to cut down?
5. How can you spend less and in which categories?

Step Two

Write down and complete fifty endings to the following sentence: "I will be satisfied when I have enough money to...." Now make a list of the things you feel you need in order to be happy in the present. Discuss your lists with your spouse and set some financial goals. Write them down and put them where you can see them on a daily basis.

Step Three

Make a list of ways that you can enjoy life and satisfy your needs without spending money. Brainstorm and write down every kind of pleasure you can access without spending money. Once you have your list, whenever you have an urge to spend money on something from one of the categories in which you tend to overspend, see if you can substitute something from your list of free pleasures.

Love Potion #27

Save some money. Write a love note to your spouse saying that the enclosed money is for spending on himself or herself. Put it somewhere your spouse will be surprised to find it. Get ready for a big kiss and hug!

The Conscious Love Revival

Spend a moment reminiscing about when you were first in love with your spouse. Do you remember how you greeted each other? How about the way you said good-bye? Like most couples, your hellos and good-byes were likely punctuated with a passionate embrace and kiss. You took each other in your arms and communicated your feelings through the physical acts of loving and kissing. And, my-oh-my, wasn't it an awesome feeling? Not only did it make you feel loved, but it most likely made you feel incredibly connected to this person.

Compare this experience to the way you say hello and good-bye to your spouse now. Do you, like so many couples, peck each other on the cheek when you say good-bye? And how about when you greet each other after a long day apart? Do you still enthusiastically communicate your love through a passionate hug and kiss? Good chance, if you have been married for more than two years, the answer is no.

So often couples wonder why they have drifted apart; why they don't have any passion left in their love relationships. One common reason is that partners stop treating each other like they did when they were first in love. They don't consciously stop doing these things; life just seems to take over and eradicate them one by one. Unfortunately, though, when the actions of love cease, the communication of love is dramatically reduced.

The good news is that if you want the passion back in your marriage, you can start by replicating the behaviors of your early relationship. As you start bringing back these loving behaviors, the feelings of passion will return as well.

For most couples, the trouble with doing this is that in order to bring back these loving behaviors they want to "feel" the love first. They think that if you don't "feel" the love, then behaving in a loving fashion is rather fake. This is understandable, since loving actions come naturally to couples when they are first in love. But this condition does not last in a relationship. It might be nice if it did, but it doesn't.

What must happen, if love is to survive, is that the couple must come to the realization that love flourishes over the long term when partners consciously treat each other in loving ways. That is, they make decisions daily to do the things that will make their spouse feel loved. When the couple starts to do this, the relationship evolves into a deeper, more mature love.

One of the best ways I know of re-kindling love in a relationship is for partners to re-visit the early stages of their love and recall the ways they communicated their love to each other. To facilitate this process, pick a time and place to relax and listen to your favorite music from when you were first in love (music greatly enhances memory). If possible, as well, recreate the sights and smells of this time. The idea is to do whatever you can to recapture the memories of how you best expressed your love to each other in the early days.

Upon recreating this time, recall for each other the things he or she did that made you feel so loved. Take turns completing this sentence: "I felt so very loved when you...." In so doing, not only will the memories come back but you may well bring a few of your lost feelings of passion to the surface. During the weeks (and years) to follow, surprise your spouse occasionally with one of the things you used to do that made him or her feel so loved in the early days.

The rule to remember here is that "feelings follow actions." If you wait around to act in a loving manner until you feel compelled by a feeling of love to do so, then you most likely will not act loving very often. The remedy is to act as if you feel all of the love you want, and then your feelings of love will come back for real.

Love Potion #28

Take your spouse in your arms when you're parting for the day and kiss him or her just like you did when you were first deeply in love. Keep the kiss up for a minimum of seven seconds. Ten is even better.

Do the same thing when you meet back at the end of the day. Do this for a month. Do it consciously even at times when you are feeling blah or stressed out. Enjoy the results!

How People *Stay* in Love

It's important to know why your spouse fell in love with you. If you have this knowledge, you can use it to help your partner stay in love with you. Everyone in a love relationship needs to help his or her spouse maintain that love. Love is not one-sided. To be loved, we must act in loving ways.

So here is the secret why your spouse fell in love with you. Your spouse first came to love you because of the way he or she felt about him- or herself in your presence. For women, it's like this: you fell in love with your husband because he said and did things that made you feel you were capable, appreciated, respected, intelligent, sexy and beautiful. For men, it's like this: you fell in love with your wife because she said and did things that made you feel capable, appreciated, respected, intelligent, sexy and handsome.

Couples that are happily married for a lifetime report that their spouses continue to make them feel such things as capable, appreciated, respected, intelligent, sexy and attractive. In other words, love is dependent on the participants in the relationship saying and doing things to make their partners feel good about themselves.

Now, I must make it clear that I strongly feel each individual in a relationship is totally responsible for his or her own happiness and self-esteem. Relying on another person for your happiness and feelings of self-worth is not a functional or healthy way to live. Rather, it's a sure way to end up both unhappy and suffering from low self-esteem. So I say in no uncertain terms that individuals must take total responsibility for themselves in these areas.

However, love is dependent on how we make the other person feel. There is no way of getting around this. The better partners make their loved ones feel in their presence the better the chance for love to exist. For love to flourish and endure, participants must continue to make each other feel good. If not, love will wane.

Some people respond to this equation rather negatively. They complain and say things like, "But I don't want to be responsible for my spouse's psychological well-being." To those who hold this view I respond with, "You only have to do this if you want to be happily married for a lifetime." While it is not fair for us to put the onus on our spouses to make us happy, it is critical to our relationships that we make our spouses feel special in every way possible.

The more things said and done to make someone feel capable, appreciated, respected, intelligent, sexy and attractive, the more a person will respond in similar fashion. This is a fact of life. Loving behavior is responded to most often with loving behavior.

There are some caveats here, though. The loving behavior cannot anticipate any reward or reciprocation. And the loving behavior must be consistent and patient. What I am saying is that if you:

1. Act in such ways to make your spouse feel capable, appreciated, respected, intelligent, sexy and attractive

2. Give your love freely without expectation of reward or reciprocation

3. You are both patient and consistent in saying and doing things to help make your spouse feel good about him- or herself, then,

4. Your spouse will feel loved, and

5. Your souse will start to act in ways that will make you feel capable, appreciated, respected, intelligent, sexy and attractive.

These are the ways that partners in long-lasting happy marriages act with each other. Couples that divorce do the opposite. Though the partners at first said and did things to make each other feel good, for one reason or another they started to say and do things that made each other feel incapable, unappreciated, disrespected, stupid, un-sexy and unattractive.

For a marriage to survive the turbulent time when passionate love wanes, at least one person in the relationship must keep love alive by continuing to make the other person feel good about him- or herself. It is, of course, better if both continue to do so. But, if not, then one at least must take the lead in order to keep the marriage together until the other can join in. Too often though, the one that takes the lead to cheer his or her partner on loses patience, gets resentful and gives up. The marriage then comes to an end.

But if you can hold on, the formula will start to work. Psychologically supporting your spouse will eventually bolster him or her, and your spouse will start to respond in kind. How long will this take? For many it can take between a month and a year. For others it can take a number of years. But, as my daddy used to say, "Honest effort is never lost." The same applies here: "Love is never lost." It will always come back to you in some fashion or other.

Love Potion #29

Designate one night a week to not watch television. Make this a "date" night. Take turns each week planning what you will do on your "date." Make some nights romantic, some relaxing and some just plain fun.

The Art of Settling Arguments: Part Three

According to the Ohio State University Medical Center, negative behaviors during marital fights affect the immune system. What are these negative behaviors that adversely affect health? They are simple ones, but they not only adversely affect health-they affect the relationship as well. The negative fighting behaviors identified in the study included: put-downs, sarcasm, interruptions, excuses and the denial of responsibility.

This is not to say that fighting is bad. Quite the contrary. Couples who learn to confront and resolve their differences have much happier marriages than couples who shun arguing.

If you are like most couples, you likely have the same arguments over and over again. And if you are like most couples, your arguments most often fall into five different categories. These are:

1. Fairness

2. Children

3. Commitment

4. Money

5. Sex

The way couples argue is of critical importance to the marriage. Some couples have fights that lead to solutions and intimacy. Others have arguments that lead to further harshness and division.

Couples who stay happily married learn to follow these rules:

The Rules of Fighting

A. Bring up the problem as soon as possible, before it becomes enormous.

B. Talk only about the issue at hand. No "throwing in the kitchen sink."

C. Stick to the present. No dredging up the past.

D. The use of definitives are not allowed (e.g., "never" and "always").

E. Verbal and physical threats are not allowed.

F. Hitting, slapping and any display of violence is strictly forbidden.

G. Needs and wants are to be stated as specific requests for different behaviors.

H. If the fight escalates, the couple is to take a minimum of 30 minutes alone to cool off. If one of the participants is really "stuck" in his or her negative feelings a cooling off period of several days may be needed. If tempers still flare, outside help should be sought before broaching the issue again.

Couples that can follow these rules have a much better chance of staying happily married than couples that consistently break them. But it isn't easy to follow these rules, and there is a very good reason why.

Anger, hurt and fear cause couples to become highly upset. When a person experiences extreme emotion, he or she gets cut off from the logical part of the brain. When a person accesses extreme emotions like anger, hurt and fear, the brain starts to shut down communication between the logical brain and the "old brain" which is directed by emotions. The "old brain" is the one that causes us to run like heck if a car is coming at us. For the sake of preservation, this brain doesn't want you to "think" about running; it just wants you to run!

This "old brain" also kicks into action when we argue. As we feel anger, hurt and fear, it overrides the logical brain and tells us to either fight or flee. So, we do what our "old brain" tells us. This is why it is so critical that the first rule of fighting be followed. If we can resolve issues early on before they get out of hand, then our feelings will not likely be strong enough to stir our "old brain" into action.

In sum, the rules of fighting require practice and patience. Arguing in such a way that you achieve both intimacy and resolution is far more an art than a science. As such, it takes years to prefect. Along the way you will experience both success and disappointments, but it will all be worth the effort.

Love Potion #30

The next time your spouse unknowingly offends you in some minor way, let go of it. Don't even mention it. Just give him or her a break. Pat yourself on the back for being a kind-hearted person and do something extra nice for him or her that day.

How Life Affects Sexual Intimacy: Part One on Sex

When couples first get married, living is normally easy. Stressful circumstances are for the most part foreign to most couples during the early years, and before children. Even careers are typically pretty tame in terms of producing stress.

Stressless times, however, do not last. Life, as it progresses, produces all kinds of stress. Much of it just seems to creep up on us. Often we are so unaware of it that when asked if we are stressed, we honestly reply with something like, "Stressed out? Me? No way. Truth is, I don't have much stress in my life at all." But it's not true. The truth may well be the exact opposite without us even realizing it.

When the flames of stress that life throws at us start to lick at our heels, our sex life also gets singed. Here is the formula to remember. The more stress in your life, the less sexual satisfaction. When it comes down to it, when couples reach the point of one or both being burdened with the problems of careers and family, they often stop having sex altogether. Or, at least, their sex life slows to such infrequency that the couple can't even remember the last time they made love.

The following fifteen statements represent common stress producers. Go over them with your spouse and give each a ranking of zero to ten depending on how true you think the statement is for you as a couple. A rank of ten would mean this area in your lives is producing a lot of stress. Zero means no stress is coming from this area whatsoever.

The Sexual Stress Test

_____ 1. One or both of us is experiencing stress at work

_____ 2. One or both of us is at odds with our parents or in-laws

____ 3. We simply do not have enough time to do everything we must do

____ 4. We have financial problems

____ 5. We do not have time for recreation

____ 6. Our children take most of our free time and attention

____ 7. Recently one or both of us experienced a major loss

____ 8. We spend very little time with friends

____ 9. One or both of us have little opportunity to be by ourselves

____ 10. We recently moved to town and now live more than 50 miles from family and friends

____ 11. One or both of us have to tend to our elderly parent's needs

____ 12. One or both of us have had an affair in the last two years

____ 13. One or both of us drinks more than three drinks a day or gets high one or more times per week

____ 14. We do not express love, appreciation and respect to and for each other on a daily basis

____ 15. One or both of us is in a transition in life

____ 16. One or both of us has significant health problems

____ 17. One or both of us is having problems with depression or another emotional problem

____ 18. One or both of us takes mood altering drugs (may be prescribed or illicit)

____   Total

Once you have totaled the score from above, come to a consensus on how satisfied you are as a couple with your sex life. (Hint: Do not base your answer on how many times you have heard it is "normal" to make love per week. Rather, base your answer on how satisfied you "emotionally feel" about your sex life.) Give it a rating from one to ten.

If you cannot come to a consensus on the number, both of you can score it from one to ten. Then, average the two scores together.

There are a couple of ways to assess the results of the Sexual Stress Test. First, if you score your satisfaction level to be seven or above, then stress is not much of a factor in your sex life. This is good. But you may want to remember this test at a more stressful time in your future.

If the two of you score your level of satisfaction less than seven and if your total score from the Sexual Stress Test is more than sixty, then stress is likely taking a toll on your sex life.

It is also possible that you may have a low total, but if you scored any of the questions above seven, then stress may also be affecting your sex life.

If stress is affecting your sex life and you are motivated to do something about it, there are several avenues of relief. These include:

1. Reducing the stress

2. Changing the way you respond to the stressor(s)

3. Finding ways to increase sexual satisfaction despite the stress

How to do these things are subjects addressed in the other chapters on sex.

Love Potion #31

The next time your spouse is experiencing emotional pain, listen carefully to his or her whole story. Get every detail and then give him or her all the sympathy you can. All of us need both understanding and sympathy at some time or another. As well, we have a need to know we are not alone in our suffering, that someone cares for us so deeply that he or she will help shield us from the harshness of the world.

Remember to give sympathy often. It is an unconditional gift of love. It will serve to fuel your love relationship so it can reach great heights.

The Friends and Foes of Sex: Part Two on Sex

"Life is difficult," says Scott Peck in his book, *The Road Less Traveled*. So is sex. Why? Well, because life is difficult. The very act of living from day to day interferes with sex. This is why sex comes so easily to young lovers. Not only is sex still erotic when a person is young, but life is so simple that it doesn't intrude into the bedroom. Truth be known, young lovers don't come out of the bedroom often enough to let life interfere!

In the chapter "How Life Affects Sexual Intimacy: Part One on Sex" three ways were offered for dealing with stress that encroaches on your sex life. These included:

1. Reducing the stress

2. Changing the way in which you respond to the stressor(s)

3. Finding ways to increase sexual satisfaction despite the stress

There is much written about how to "turn on" your spouse, but in my estimation, most all couples already know how to do this. I'm not saying that it's not good to learn about and explore new and different ways to please each other, because these are good things to do. I am saying, though, that as long as stress is intruding into the bedroom, sex will likely be lack-luster, infrequent and unsatisfying.

But there are some relatively easy things that can help to immediately mitigate the adverse affects of stress on your sex life. Here are a few you might consider:

1. Go to Bed earlier. Stress is much easier dealt with if both partners are well rested. Also, tiredness zaps people of sexual desire.

2. Put a lock on the bedroom door if you have children. This will reduce the stress that comes from the fear that a child may walk in at the wrong moment.

3. Take a short trip, even if it's just for the weekend, and go somewhere alone. Sex thrives away from home.

4. Establish a pattern of listening and showing empathy to each other. Not only do listening and empathy lower stress levels but they also increase feelings of love and passion.

5. Take a course on stress or buy a good book on the subject. If you keep on dealing with stress the same way you've always dealt with stress, you will likely continue to be stressed out.

6. Go to a big bookstore. Find the section on relationships. Somewhere in this section will be a number of books on sex. Pick one out together, go home, put on some romantic music and read the book aloud to each other. Do what the book says.

7. Put just as much effort into being loving after sex that you put into being loving before sex. This will bolster each other's confidence to go out and handle the stress at hand. It will also reinforce sexual desire for the next time around.

All of these things together and separately can help couples recover the satisfaction they once had in the early days of their love. If they don't help, there are several possibilities that need to be examined. Ask yourselves these questions:

A. Is one area of stress overwhelming you? If the stress is transitional, then be patient and wait for it to pass. In the meantime, have patience and put your sex life on hold. If the stress is ongoing, then you will need to either find a way to change your circumstances or figure out how to handle the stress differently.

B. How is your relationship? One of the great foes of good sex is a lousy relationship. If each partner does not feel capable, appreciated, respected, intelligent, sexy and attractive, then sexual satisfaction will diminish markedly. Fix the relationship and sexual satisfaction will return.

C. Do either of you have any physical problems? Physical conditions often affect sex tremendously; both desire and sexual function can be adversely affected. If one or both of you are having any of these kinds of problems, talk with your physician about it. There may well be a very simple cure. Also, consider making an appointment with a clinic that specializes in sexuality. Most large cities have them and they will have all of the most up-to-date methods to both diagnose and treat your problem.

Like all the other areas of marriage, sex is one that must be attended to and worked on. Thinking that sex should always be like it was "in the beginning" is counter- productive. This kind of attitude never leads to more sexual satisfaction. Rather, it can lead to affairs and divorce.

Couples that stay happily married for a lifetime do what it takes to build and maintain a sex life that satisfies the needs of both partners. You can too. One thing is clear, though. A satisfying sex life takes lots of work and lots of patience. And like so many other areas of marriage, the levels of satisfaction can vary dramatically depending on how much "life" is intruding into the bedroom.

Love Potion #32

Plan an hour of lovemaking. Put your favorite music on and burn either some incense or candles. Take turns giving each other pleasure at ten-minute intervals. When it is the "receiver's" turn, this person's only responsibility is to enjoy and give feedback; he or she is not to give pleasure. After ten minutes, switch roles. Do this back and forth until each of you have had three turns at both giving and receiving. (Hint: If one or both of you reach an orgasm, relax for a few minutes and go back to it).

Putting the Sparkle Back: Part Three on Sex

If you have been married for more than two years then the automatic sparkle that comes with young love is likely to have worn off. As a shiny new car eventually loses its sparkle, so do marital relationships.

During the early days of marriage, the partners upon seeing each other go kind of "gaga." Adrenaline courses through their veins, heartbeats quicken, blood pressures rise and loving feelings swell. Each person feels intensely alert and hypersensitive to the other's touch and smell. Every sense, every part of the body responds. What they're feeling is what we call "love." There's nothing like it!

And in the bedroom, WOW! Sensitivity for each other reaches a crescendo. The intensity of love reaches its peak. Physical passion when added to the emotional feeling of love makes a powerful elixir. It is the stuff that forms the basis for marital relationships to begin their growth.

While it would seem wonderful for a couple to continue to live in this state of bliss, it is not meant to be. The routines of daily living, familiarity and predictability start to take their toll. As time goes on, not by design or choice, when couples see each other heartbeats no longer accelerate, blood pressures don't rise and feelings of love don't swell. In time, as well, body responses normalize and the "wow" goes away.

But, on a positive note, love between the partners has now taken root and been fertilized by passion. Once this happens, the seeds have been strewn for the growth of a more permanent, stable and mature love. This is absolutely necessary if a couple is to be happily married for a lifetime. But it's also necessary to once in a while do what it takes to rekindle the passion of early love.

Re-igniting the flames of early love is necessary for two reasons. The first is because the automatic passion of early marriage always fades and has no capacity to regenerate itself. If passion is to survive in a marriage, the partners will have to consciously do what is necessary to keep it. Second, consciously keeping the excitement in your sex life is necessary because love wanes if you don't. Sex is a powerful bonding agent in a marriage. To not pay attention to it is to let one of the central fetters of marriage shrivel and fade away from neglect.

One of the most destructive myths of marriage is that if passion fades then love has been lost. The conclusion that follows is what makes the myth so damaging to the marriage: that is, "I no longer feel passion for my spouse so I need to go find someone else to love." Once this conclusion is drawn, a person is ripe to fall into the trap of a heated affair, during which he or she further concludes, "I was right. I again feel passionate love again, so I should get a divorce and marry my true love." These inferences cause a good number of the one million annual American divorces.

All of these reasons are very good ones to put time and effort into keeping passion alive and well in your marriage. Here are several suggestions that will help you put the spark back in your marriage.

1. Buy a book or take a course in massage together. Practice on each other frequently. Touching and giving are two things that stir up the coals of passion.

2. Go to bed, turn out the lights and ask your partner what things he or she absolutely likes best when making love. Take turns putting them into action.

3. Ask your partner to name five things that turn him or her on. Make note of them and put them into practice.

4. Go buy a copy of 101 Nights of Great Sex by Laura Corn or Soulful Sex: Opening Your Heart, Body and Spirit to Lifelong Passion by Victoria Lee, or get a copy of The Joys of Sex. Study the contents together, in bed.

5. Brainstorm together how you can involve all five senses in your love-making.

6. Ask your mate what his or idea of the perfect romantic evening is. Make it a reality.

7. Kiss your spouse passionately in the morning. Call to say "I love you" during the day, kiss your spouse passionately when you get back together in the evening and verbalize your desire to make love that night.

Love Potion #33

Decide on a place in the house that is very accessible on a moment's notice for stealing private time together. Use this as your "Kissing Place." Go there often, at least once a day. (Hint: The more you use your Kissing Place, the livelier and more satisfying your sex life will be!)

Kiss and Tell: Part One

How well do you really know your spouse? Most married people answer this question with something like, "Very well. In fact, I know my spouse better than he/she does." No matter how well you know your spouse, there is a lot more to know. The good thing is that happily married partners say they never tire of getting to know their spouses better.

The chapters in the book titled "Kiss and Tell" will be devoted to helping you discover more about your spouse. You can expect this process of discovery to be an extraordinarily powerful one. Not only will you be pleased to uncover a number of exciting things about your spouse, but you will also, in the process of asking and listening, bolster and cement the bond of love between you.

In a number of places in this book I talk about the fact that for love to flourish, each person must feel capable, appreciated, respected, intelligent, sexy and attractive. One of the most powerful ways I know for couples to communicate these things to each other is by asking important questions and attentively listening to the answers.

So, in the Kiss and Tell chapters, I've included questions for you to ask of your spouse. The more you ask, the better you will come to know your spouse and the better he or she will feel about him or herself. Both of you will benefit by increased feelings of love and compassion.

Kiss and Tell Instructions:

1. Flip a coin to see who goes first. The winner decides whether to Kiss or Tell first.

2. The Kisser gives the Teller a kiss (preferably passionate) and picks a question to ask.

3. The Kisser listens while following The Rules of Listening (see the chapter "The Art of Arguing: Part One").

4. The Teller answers the questions to the best of his or her ability.

5. Switch roles. The new kisser can choose to ask the same question or a different one.

6. Keep a sense of humor and use it often. Laughing and all forms of encouragement are strongly suggested.

Kiss and Tell Questions

1. What attracted you to me the first time we met?

2. What is a favorite tradition of yours from your childhood?

3. Do you ever have crazy thoughts? If so, what do you do about them?

4. What do you fear most?

5. Have you ever been able to overcome a fear? If so, how did you do it?

6. What do you think are your best features? Your worst?

7. If you could have one super power, what would you choose and why?

8. What is the smartest thing you have ever done outside of marrying me?

9. What was your most embarrassing moment in childhood? How did it affect your life?

10. Would you rather continue doing what you are doing with most of your time, or would you rather do something else? Why or what?

11. Which feelings are easy for you to express and which are hard? Why?

12. What thoughts does the statement, "It is more important to understand than to be understood" bring to your mind? How do you think it applies to marriage?

Love Potion #34

Make love in every room of your house. Don't forget your closets, laundry room and staircases. Be creative. Take your time. Make each time and place an unforgettable experience. Take turns creating the experience for different rooms. Name the room and time and set a date to meet there.

Kiss and Tell: Part Two

If you asked and answered some of the questions in "Kiss and Tell-Part One", you are likely looking forward to Part Two. Getting to know each other can be a highly positive addiction. The process draws people closely together; even closer than they were during the early days of their love.

Here are the instructions again. Change them, if you wish, to suit your purposes and relationship, especially if it will make the process of Kissing and Telling more fun.

Kiss and Tell Instructions:

1. Flip a coin to see who goes first. The winner decides whether to Kiss or Tell first.

2. The Kisser gives the Teller a kiss (preferably passionate) and picks a question to ask.

3. The Kisser listens following The Rules of Listening (see the chapter "The Art of Arguing: Part One").

4. The Teller answers all the questions to the best of his or her ability.

5. Switch roles. The new kisser can choose to ask the same question or a different one.

6. Keep a sense of humor and use it often. Laughing and all forms of encouragement are strongly suggested.

Kiss and Tell Questions: Part Two

1. Which of your senses is the most acute? Which the least?

2. If you could have the body of a movie star, whose would you pick and why?

3. What are your three fondest memories of us being together?

4. What are the three things you value most about our relationship?

5. Whose marriage do you admire most? Why?

6. Whose marriage do you think is the worst? Why?

7. What does being intimate mean to you?

8. What is the single most important ingredient of a happy marriage?

9. What are four habits you wish you could change? How would you benefit from these changes?

10. What is one thing you would like me to change about myself? Why?

11. What is the best thing about you? The worst?

12. What do you think is your most important contribution to our relationship?

Love Potion #35

Cook a gourmet meal together on Saturday evening. During the week plan everything from the menu to the music and the centerpiece for the table. Either arrange for the children to be out of the house, or plan to eat after the children are in bed. Eat by candlelight and enjoy!

More Communication Mistakes That Can Make a Disaster of Your Marriage

I asked my wife, Nydia, one day at lunch what she felt was the most important ingredient of a happy marriage. She said, "Well, if I had to pick one thing, I would say it's communication." When I asked why, she replied, "Because everything depends on communication. I mean communication is a daily affair. You can't do it one day and not the next. You constantly have to talk with your spouse. If you do it badly, nothing else will go right either."

Smart person, my wife. She put the critical nature of communication succinctly. The quality of communication in a marriage determines the quality of the relationship. They are in direct relation to each other.

This is not good news for many couples. For some, the wish is that somehow the marriage will work if they make enough money or focus on the kids or become successful in their careers or if they have a great sex life. Sorry. None of these will matter much if the partners don't lick their communication problems.

But how do you know if you have a communication problem in your marriage? Most often it is easy. Just listen to your spouse. If you have a problem, he or she has most likely been telling you about it for quite a while. But because of the communication problem, you most likely have not "heard" or at least believed what he or she has been saying. So you may not know whether or not you have a problem, or if you do, the severity of it. Here is a test you and your spouse can take to help determine if you have a problem. It will also give you an indication of the severity of the communication problem.

The Communication Test

Instructions: Give the following questions a score between zero and ten. If you feel your spouse never does this, score it a zero. If he or she does it a lot, score it a ten. Or, score it somewhere between the two depending on how you would rank the frequency or severity of the behavior. Make sure to score the test based on your spouse's communication behavior, not your own.

_____1. My spouse does not stop and look at me when I am talking

_____2. Sometimes my spouse ridicules what I say

_____3. My mate often tries to talk me into changing my feelings

_____4. Sometimes my spouse calls me names

_____5. When I try to talk about problems, my spouse tries to change the subject

_____6. My spouse always has an excuse

_____7. Often my husband/wife pouts if I bring up problems

_____8. When my spouse and I argue I often end up feeling demeaned

_____9. My spouse is prone to making exaggerations

_____10. My spouse makes up lies or tells half-truths

_____11. My spouse is dogmatic

_____12. My spouse insists on looking at things logically

_____13. My spouse won't listen to me if I look at things logically

_____14. My spouse loses his/her temper when we argue

_____15. My partner blows me off

_____16. If I don't give in to my spouse, he/she won't give me any peace until I do

_____17. My partner likes to play psychologist with me (analyzes my motives)

_____18. My spouse brings up past mistakes when we argue

_____19. My spouse refuses to take any responsibility

_____20. My spouse knows my "hot buttons" and doesn't hesitate to push them

To score this test, look and see if you scored any of the items over a five. If so, your communication with your spouse is less than ideal and needs work. This is not uncommon, so don't feel bad about it. What is common in marriages is to have several areas that need work. Most of this work can be accomplished relatively easily if both partners are open to giving and receiving honest feedback and to making commitments to change. The exercises in the chapters titled "The Art of Arguing" will help.

However, if you scored a number of items eight or above, your communication problem may well be severe enough to warrant outside help. There should be no shame in seeking outside help. Communication problems can be horrendously destructive in relationships. In the process of communicating badly, anger, hurt and resentment can build to intolerable levels. Without help these feelings can be virtually insurmountable. If you feel this is the case with you, before you call a divorce lawyer, call a marriage counselor.

To find a good marriage counselor, ask around. Ask your friends, pastor or rabbi, or doctor which marriage counselors in your area get good results. Try, if you can, to find someone who is licensed and who specializes in marriage counseling. If at first you don't find someone who can help you, try someone else. (Hint: When people have a physical problem, they go to a doctor. If that doctor doesn't get results, they find another that can).

Love Potion #36

Change one bad habit you know annoys your spouse. Just one. Commit to trying the change for one month. If the habit annoys your spouse, it is likely a nuisance to you at some level as well. So, for one month stop smoking, eat less, stop drinking, exercise better manners, work less, dress better or eat better. Whatever it is, just do it!

Assessing the Strength of Your Marriage

A recent report out of the University of Wisconsin said that marriages formed since 1985 are failing at the rate of 67%. Commitment to marriage, one would assume from this statistic, is at an all-time low. This is too bad for many reasons.

For marriage to work there must be a commitment to the long term. The problem is, there are many ups and downs in marriages and if there is no commitment to the long-term, couples will pull out of the marriage during one of the down times. In a way, this makes as much sense as cashing in mutual funds during a down time in the stock market. Everyone knows that in order to make money in the stock market, investments must be committed to in the long term. Pull your money out too soon and likely you will lose. And not only will you lose your money, you'll get really stressed out, if you're trying to decide each day whether or not you should leave your money in or take it out.

The same goes for marriage. Marriage pays off in the long run. However, on any single day, satisfaction may either be up or down. At some point in a marriage, in order for sanity and stability to prevail, the partners must decide that they are going to stay together for the long term. Even though most couples take marriage vows "till death do us part," there still comes a time in a marriage when the couple must consciously reaffirm that they are going to stay together despite problems and disappointments.

Here is a self-test which will help you assess the level of commitment you have in your marriage.

Commitment and Dedication Assessment Test

Instructions: Score the following statements from one to ten depending on how true you think the statement is about yourself. A one is the lowest score and a ten the highest. Total your score at the bottom. For privacy, score your answers on another sheet of paper.

_____1. When I come across something that is going to affect me, I also consider how it will affect us as a couple.

_____2. When I view the long term, I see my spouse and me married in our retirement.

_____3. I often sacrifice my own wants and needs if it will benefit my marriage.

_____4. While I may fantasize about someone else, I am not seriously attracted to anyone but my spouse.

_____5. I have a strong desire to maintain my marriage despite the difficult times.

_____6. My marriage is one of the most important things in my life.

_____7. Rarely do I think about what it would be like to be married to someone else.

_____8. My relationship comes first.

_____9. My vision for the future includes my spouse.

_____10. I get joy out of making sacrifices for my mate.

_____ Total

The total possible points are 100. On average, couples that report their marriages to be both happy and stable score about 83 points on this test. If your score is similar then you are also dedicated to staying in your marriage. If you scored below a sixty-four, then your level of commitment to your marriage is low in your eyes.

Whatever your score was, consider how your attitudes about commitment may affect the future of your marriage.

Love Potion #37

Plan a ceremony to reaffirm your marriage vows. It can be anything from a simple private ceremony with just the two of you to a major event with guests and a party afterwards. In either case, go to the library or bookstore and ask for a book on planning weddings. In it you will get some great ideas on how to make your ceremony special and meaningful to you. (Hint: A second honeymoon after the ceremony would be nice as well. If you can't plan a major trip, plan a special evening in town.)

Do You Need a Marriage Counselor?

Before going on, take this self-quiz. (Hint: Do not read ahead. Reading the comments will skew the results.)

Put an X by the traits that you feel describe your spouse. Be honest. Mark both the positive and the negative. For privacy, use a separate sheet to record your answers.

Partner Description Inventory

_____ Kind	_____ Dishonest
_____ Modest	_____ Inviting
_____ Grateful	_____ Hateful
_____ Dangerous	_____ Forthright
_____ Thrifty	_____ Forgiving
_____ Tense	_____ Logical
_____ Agreeable	_____ Sanctimonious
_____ Blatant	_____ Stable
_____ Dogmatic	_____ Overbearing
_____ Sensitive	_____ Creative
_____ Unforgiving	_____ Altruistic
_____ Inappropriate	_____ Dependable
_____ Playful	_____ Gentle
_____ Caring	_____ Childish
_____ Complimentary	_____ Philosophical

_____ Jealous	_____ Careful
_____ Open	_____ Intrusive
_____ Shy	_____ Insensitive
_____ Warm	_____ Righteous
_____ Annoying	_____ Inflexible
_____ Available	_____ Interested
_____ Open-minded	_____ Depressed
_____ Giving	_____ Soothing
_____ Connected	_____ Self-confident
_____ Arrogant	_____ Exact
_____ Persuasive	_____ Conscious
_____ Assured	_____ Unconscious
_____ Weak	_____ Loving
_____ Critical	_____ Thoughtful
_____ Self-assured	_____ Mild-mannered
_____ Stingy	_____ Inappropriate
_____ Fair	_____ Patient
_____ Supportive	_____ Impatient
_____ Complimentary	_____ Unreliable
_____ Trusting	_____ Accountable
_____ Encouraging	_____ Spontaneous
_____ Forgiving	_____ Controlled
_____ Unyielding	_____ Uncontrolled
_____ Fragile	_____ Spiritual
_____ Giving	_____ Brash
_____ Boorish	_____ Bright
_____ Available	_____ Dull

_____ Imaginative   _____ Appreciative

_____ Objective   _____ Selfish

_____ Controlling   _____ Wise

_____ Inviting   _____ Intelligent

_____ Discouraging   _____ Sincere

_____ Cold   _____ Amiable

_____ Precise   _____ Friendly

_____ Good-natured

Now that you have marked the characteristics that your spouse has in your eyes, go back and mark which ones are positive and which ones are negative. Put a P by the positive ones and an N by the negative ones. (Hint: To determine which are the positive and which are the negatives, use your own opinion. If the trait is admirable to you, mark it positive, if it is something you wish your spouse would change then mark it negative.)

Once you have designated which are the positive and which are negative, go back and total up how many positive and how many negative there are.

The total number does not matter. What matters is the prevailing way you view your spouse. In happy marriages, couples view each other to have, for the most part, positive traits. This does not mean that they don't recognize some of their partner's faults. On the contrary, they are aware of their partner's failings but in total see them to be outweighed by the good traits.

Ask a couple who is headed to divorce court to take this same test and each will come up with a list that is loaded with the negative. If this same couple had taken the test near the beginning of the marriage, the results would have been heavy on the positive. At some point in the marriage, two things happened. First, the blinders of early love came off and the faults that were already there became consciously recognizable. Second, the stresses of life started to intrude into the relationship and each person started to react to them in his or her own way, either positive or negative. Over time, character traits are revealed to each other.

A third thing happens in the process as well. That is, each person in the marriage starts to view the other in either a positive or negative light. Once the focus is chosen, evidence is sought out and reported. For example, if a positive focus is decided upon, then a person will find evidence to support the conclusion that his or her spouse has positive traits. In turn, this person reports that positive evidence to his or her spouse. At the same time, evidence to the contrary is either downplayed or ignored.

It goes something like this. A husband notices his wife is neat and organized. He decides this is a positive trait. Then he points out the evidence to his spouse of how neat and organized she is and expresses appreciation for it. When he notices a time when she is sloppy or disorganized, he either ignores it or rationalizes it away as an aberration.

The opposite happens if a decision has been reached that the spouse has negative traits. In the same scenario, the husband notices his wife is neat and organized. He decides this is a negative trait. He, in turn, interprets the time spent cleaning to be obsessive and complains to his wife that she is a "neat-freak." At a time when she is sloppy, he ignores it or rationalizes it away as an aberration.

What is important here is the focus that is chosen. Whichever focus is taken will determine the level of happiness in the marriage. The level of happiness, in turn, most likely will determine whether or not the couple stays together. Also, couples that choose a positive focus reinforce each other's positive traits. Couples with a negative focus reinforce each other's negative traits. So, behavior in the marriage gets either better or worse, depending on whether the couple has a positive or negative focus.

If one or both of you have a negative focus, it will likely be very tough for you to turn this around without help. If the marriage is to survive and be happy, then outside help should be sought from a qualified marriage counselor. Getting help requires putting your ego aside and investing both time and money. But think of it this way: Divorce is a much bigger blow to the ego, your time and your pocket book than marriage counseling will ever be.

Love Potion #38

Send your spouse a gift at work. It doesn't matter what it is, but make it visual and showy. The idea is to create a big stir among his or her work mates. Envy is the name of the game. Go for a lot of "oohs and ahs." This will do wonders for helping your spouse feel cared about and appreciated. Enjoy the rewards at home that night!

Do You Feel Bad?

Most people tend to find positive emotions easy to identify and express. Negative emotions are another matter. Many people have trouble identifying them, and some will go out of their way to avoid expressing them.

There is a good reason for this. Negative feelings often beget negative reactions. If a person has experienced negative reactions to the expression of negative feelings, he or she will likely be reticent to express them. These experiences can be either personal or vicarious.

In addition, many people have never had an adequate role model for expressing negative emotions. The result is that not only do they not know how to express them, but they also have no idea how to identify and name these feelings.

Rectifying this takes motivation, information and practice.

If you don't learn to tell your partner how you're feeling verbally, the feelings will either (a) come out "sideways" or (b) pile up until they erupt in an angry outburst. An example of "coming out sideways" is when a person is angry about something and, instead of expressing the anger verbally, refuses to do something the other person wants. Another phrase for this is "passive aggressive behavior." Anger expressed in such a way tremendously undermines a marriage.

Controlling negative emotions, or "keeping them in," also has a deleterious effect on a marriage. Pent-up emotions have energy, and this energy has a negative charge. It takes additional energy to hold these emotions in; the more negative emotions that are "stuffed" the more energy it takes to hold them in. This robs a person of energy he or she could use for productive persons. Also, anger turned inward often becomes depression or takes a toll on the person's physical health.

Ultimately, the risk in stuffing feelings is that a person can only hold in so much. When a person reaches his or her limit, the slightest thing can cause all of the negative emotions to flood out. If this happens, watch out. Not only do the emotions come out, but they also get expressed with all the energy that's attached to them. An example: A husband forgets to take out the garbage and the wife responds with outrage. The sheer force of her anger blows him away and she will not (or cannot) hear anything he has to say, not even an apology.

Understanding these dynamics will help motivate you to express your emotions as they come up, but you expressing them still takes some knowledge and practice.

Here is a list of negative emotions that can help you identify your feelings. The next time you're feeling "bad" but can't quite put your finger on the specific emotion, refer to this list.

Negative Feeling List

_____ Angry	_____ Dominated
_____ Repulsed	_____ Excluded
_____ Cowardly	_____ Hopeless
_____ Hate	_____ Sad
_____ Gutless	_____ Discouraged
_____ Animosity	_____ Ostracized
_____ Nervous	_____ Abandoned
_____ Cold	_____ Rejected
_____ Fearful	_____ Distant
_____ Indifferent	_____ Withdrawn
_____ Afraid	_____ Invisible
_____ Bored	_____ Ignored
_____ Sorrowful	_____ Suppressed
_____ Annoyed	_____ Disapproved of

____ Lonely	____ Helpless
____ Humiliated	____ Humiliated
____ Disgusted	____ Uneasy
____ Anxious	____ Hopeless
____ Remorseful	____ Distrustful
____ Guilty	____ Hurt
____ Disappointed	____ Devalued
____ Disgusted	____ Inadequate
____ Enraged	____ Cheated
____ Smothered	____ Depressed
____ Shameful	____ Remorseful
____ Blamed	____ Trapped
____ Embarrassed	____ Insecure
____ Inadequate	____ Cheated
____ Cheated	

Identifying your feelings is requisite to being able to express them. But even when you have a feeling pegged, it can be difficult to verbalize it to your spouse. This is especially true if your feeling is a result of something he or she said or did. When this is the case, people often fear rejection or conflict will result if they verbalize their feelings. Still, in order to avoid the potential destruction that can result from holding feelings back, it is necessary to take the risk of verbalizing them.

Here is a good way to practice. Working privately, sit down with a pad of paper and pen. Think of at least three circumstances that cause you to feel bad. Refer to the Negative Feeling List and identify what you feel. Then, using the F-N-W formula write down what you feel, what you need, and what you want. An example would be: "I feel ignored when you read the paper at breakfast. I need your attention. I want you to talk to me at breakfast and not read the paper." Write at least three of these statements down.

When you feel comfortable, take a risk and share one of your statements with your spouse. (Hint: Choose something fairly innocuous and do it at a time when emotions are not running too high.) Have some patience with yourself. The first few times you may make some mistakes. Keep at it, though, and you will become an expert at verbalizing both your feelings and your needs.

Love Potion #39

Order something from your spouse's favorite catalog. Keep it a secret. Play "dumb" when it arrives.

Do You Feel Good?

Do you feel good a lot of the time? Does your spouse say and do things that make you feel capable, appreciated, respected, intelligent, sexy and attractive? If so, are you good at expressing your appreciation and giving positive feedback?

Sometimes, partners take their spouses' giving behaviors for granted. When confronted, unaware of their sins of omission, they say something like, "My spouse already knows how much I appreciate everything he/she does. There is no need to keep saying thank you."

Wrong! Behavior that goes unappreciated diminishes. One of the most common complaints in marriages is lack of appreciation. The odd thing is that while each human being has a need to be appreciated for his or her contributions, human beings tend to be lackadaisical in their efforts to give the very thing they so badly want given to them.

In long-standing happy marriages, appreciation is expressed on a regular if not daily basis by both partners. Here is a way to express your appreciation in a sincere way that is sure to convey your appreciation to your spouse.

To clearly communicate to your spouse that you are appreciative, use the F-N-W formula. Pick out something your mate does that really makes you feel good, decide what need it fills, and identify what you want. It would go something like this: "When you come home and kiss me, I feel loved. I need to feel loved by you and I want you to kiss me every day." Or, "I feel grateful when you take time to listen to my problems at work. I need to have someone to talk to about what I'm going through. I want you to keep listening to me. It makes a big difference to me."

Here is a list of positive feelings to refer to. It can help you express exactly how you are feeling to your spouse.

The Positive Feeling List

____ Cheerful	____ Independent
____ Determined	____ Encouraged
____ Resolute	____ Spirited
____ Enthusiastic	____ Peaceful
____ Certain	____ Ecstatic
____ Surprised	____ Respected
____ Affectionate	____ Appreciated
____ Calm	____ Attractive
____ Exhilarated	____ Capable
____ Refreshed	____ Inspired
____ Elated	____ Creative
____ Excited	____ Debonair
____ Curious	____ Frisky
____ Brave	____ Fascinated
____ Confident	____ Silly
____ Sexy	____ Proud
____ Strong	____ Pleased
____ Intelligent	____ Comfortable
____ Lighthearted	____ Energetic
____ Carefree	____ Festive
____ Loving	____ Tranquil
____ Lively	____ Thankful
____ Respectful	____ Tuned on
____ Playful	____ Earnest
____ Jubilant	____ Bold
____ Courageous	____ Reassured

Love Potion #40

Write your spouse a love note. Put it in a book he or she is reading

What Does Your Spouse Expect of You?

When two people get married, they have expectations of each other. Yet neither is typically aware of his or her own expectations or the expectations of the partner. As my daddy used to say, "This is a fine kettle of fish." Of course, what he meant was that this set of circumstances is a mess, and it's going to be difficult to clean up.

In long-term happy marriages, partners sort through and come to know each other's expectations. As they became aware of them, negotiations take place and modifications are made to the expectations. This process, as you might imagine, takes years, lots of patience, flexibility, understanding and even some forgiveness.

Rather than hope time will eventually reveal expectations, it is wise to take a more proactive approach. Consciously identifying and communicating expectations can save a lot of hurt feelings and can help both partners get their needs met.

To help you become more conscious of your expectations, here are a set of questions for you to ask each other.

Expectation Exploration Questions

Instructions: In doing this exercise, use the rules of communication found in the chapter titled "The Art of Arguing: Part One." If you feel one of your spouse's expectations is unreasonable or is an expectation you are unwilling to meet, hold back your response until you ask questions and fully understand why and where your spouse is coming from. After doing this, in a compassionate (and non-defensive way) let your spouse know of your objection. Help your partner discover what need this expectation might be motivated by. Then, brainstorm and negotiate some other ways for the need to be met.

Take turns asking and answering each question. Take some time with this exercise. You may even want to revisit it on several occasions.

1. What are your expectations regarding children? How many do you want? Will we both work or will one stay home to care for the children? If so, for how long?

2. Whose career comes first? Will we both work, or only one of us?

3. How should we handle money? Who will pay the bills? Who will balance the checkbook? How will we decide on long-term investments?

4. How often do you expect we will have sex? Who should initiate it? Are there any taboos?

5. What are your expectations regarding friends? Is it okay to spend time alone with friends? If so, how much time and doing what kinds of things?

6. What are your views on divorce? Do you think it is possible that we might one day divorce? What kinds of things do you think could cause us to divorce?

7. What are your views on monogamy? Do you think it is okay to have an "open marriage"? Why or why not?

8. How do you think we should handle problems that come up? What should we do if one of us becomes extremely angry with the other?

9. What are your views on forgiveness? In marriage, are there any behaviors you feel that are totally unforgivable?

10. What expectations do you have for our family in regard to religion and spirituality? What religious practices are important to you? How do you view a parent's role in spiritually guiding his/her children?

11. What little things irritate you? What are your expectations regarding them?

12. In regard to our free time, what are your expectations about "together time" and "alone time"?

13. What are your expectations of sleep time? Is it okay to wake you up if I have a problem to discuss? How about sleeping extra on weekends and holidays? What about going to bed at different times?

14. What are your expectations regarding household tasks? Who should do what?

15. Who is in charge? Will we share control or will each of us control certain things like money and disciplining the children? What happens if we can't come to an agreement on an issue?

16. Do you think it is more important to be friends or lovers? What does it mean for marriage partners to be friends? To be lovers? To be both?

Love Potion #41

Pick a specific time of day. It can be any time. Agree to stop and think of each other at that time for one minute. Think loving, uplifting thoughts and end it with a prayer for the other's well-being. (Hint: Figure out some way to remind yourself. If you do forget, do it as soon as you remember.)

The Boomerang Effect

The Boomerang Effect happens when one partner shares something of a personal nature and the other uses it against him or her in a future fight. The whole thing goes something like this.

Let's say Lonnie is having some trouble at work. His boss is really on his case. Lonnie comes home to tell his tale of woe to his wife, Cheryl, who is very understanding. Cheryl, in fact, listens and empathizes so well that Lonnie keeps talking until he comes to an insight that his boss has just cause to be on his case because of his lack of organization. Lonnie even admits to goofing off a bit lately.

Fast-forward two weeks. Cheryl and Lonnie are fighting at home over household chores. Cheryl tells Lonnie that the real problem is that he is disorganized and likes to goof off. As proof, she points to the problem at work. If the fight escalates she might even throw in something like, "Lonnie, you're so lazy and disorganized I wouldn't be surprised if you lost your job. I'm not going to put up with it any more than your boss!" At this point Lonnie explodes with, "I'm never telling you any of my problems again. You just use them against me!" At which time he storms out of the room.

Any feelings and/or thoughts shared in trust in a marriage must be kept sacrosanct. To use them at a later date to condemn the other person is to undermine trust. And if you take the trust out of the marriage, you remove a major part of the foundation of the marriage.

As tempting as it can be in the heat of battle to use any and all means to win your point, all information gained in a moment of sharing must not be used. If you use it, it may help you win the proverbial "battle" but you will also speed the losing of the "war."

Love Potion #42

In marriage, if you always wait until you "feel" like doing something, you will end up doing less and less over time. So, practice taking action when your feelings are saying, "Nah, I'd rather not." Here are some things to practice on.

* making love when you are oh, so tired

* going to church when the covers have a warm grip on you

* listening when you are preoccupied with your own problems

Is Your Spouse Still in Love with You?

In the United States of America, somewhat over one million couples get divorced each year. In some of these divorces, one of the partners, over time, became totally disenchanted with the marriage while the other thought all was well.

When you talk to the person who became disenchanted, he or she typically says something like, "I tried to tell my spouse for years that I wasn't happy, that things needed to change. But he/she just wouldn't listen. Oh, yeah, we would talk a little bit, but nothing would ever change. He/she would just blow me off. Nothing would get resolved. I'm tired of it. This isn't how I want to live the rest of my life. There has to be something better out there and I'm going to go find it."

If you talk to this person's spouse, he or she says something like, "I never knew my spouse was so unhappy. I just don't understand it. I thought things were just fine. Sure, we would have our little fights but we would get over them and things would go on. But we didn't have any major fights. If he/she was so unhappy, I wish something would have been said sooner. Now I'm being blamed for the marriage falling apart and I don't even know what I did."

Conversations like these take place in marriage counselors' and divorce lawyers' offices thousands of times each year. If the words are not identical, the thoughts are. One person feels like he or she is in a loveless marriage while the other is both generally satisfied and oblivious to the other's discontent.

The pertinent question for you, then, is "Are you sure your spouse is still in love with you?" This is a question you should not answer yourself. It is a question you need to ask your mate. And I would suggest that you don't just ask whether or not he or she loves you. Rather, ask some probing questions that will give you a better idea of your mate's level of marital satisfaction.

If asking questions that may stir up problem areas seems risky to you, then you already have one indication that "all is not well in paradise." It is far better to get things out into the open so you can deal with them than it is to stay in denial and hope the problems will go away. They won't. Time does not heal problems. People heal problems. And the only way to heal them is to be aware of them.

At least once a year, couples should check up on each other's level of satisfaction with the other and with the marriage. An analogy here is going to the dentist for a check-up. It may be a real bother. It may even lead to finding some decay which in turn leads to the painful process of a root canal. However, this pain is temporary and manageable. If, on the other hand, the check-up is not done, the decay will not be discovered right away. When the decay grows to a point that it causes pain so intense that it can no longer be ignored, it may be too late. The tooth may be lost regardless of your desire to save it.

Like teeth, all marriages have problems once in a while. And, like teeth, these problems will not heal themselves. Before the problems in either can be taken care of, they must first be identified. Here are some questions to help you do a check-up on your marriage. When you ask them, it would be wise to be non-defensive and to use the rules of communication.

The 12 Marital Check-Up Questions

1. How do you feel about the amount of time we spend together?

2. Is there anything you would like to change about the things we do together?

3. What do you think about our sex life? Is it satisfying to you? What would you like for us to change?

4. Do you feel like I support you? Is there something I could do to support you better?

5. Do you feel like I do my share of household tasks? Is there something you would like to see me do differently?

6. How do you feel about the amount of love and affection we express to each other? Is there anything you would like us to change in this area?

7. What, if anything, do you think we ought to change about the way we handle our finances?

8. What are your greatest pleasures in life? Are you getting enough pleasure? If not, how can I support your getting more?

9. What is your greatest hope for our future?

10. How do you feel about the number and types of gifts that I give you?

11. When thinking about the way we communicate, are there any changes you would like to see made?

12. Do I say and do things to help you feel: Capable? Appreciated? Respected? Intelligent? Sexy? Attractive?

By the time each of you have asked and listened to the other's responses to The 12 Marital Check-Up Questions, you will have a good idea of the "State of Your Marriage." You will also know what changes need to be made. Knowing these things is vital to keeping a marriage together.

Here are two cautions. Once you know about the changes your spouse is asking of you and you have agreed to the changes, then you must make an honest effort to make those changes. To make commitments to change without following through is to also undermine your marriage. Perfect change is not required for a marriage to be happy, but an honest effort is!

It is also wise to keep in mind that people's needs and desires change. What once was perfectly acceptable may now be completely unacceptable. Therefore, is advisable to do these check-ups at least yearly. When you do so, do not be shocked if the answers change.

Love Potion #43

Use your creativity to write down the following Bible verse in such a way that you could frame it and hang it up where the two of you couldn't help but see it every day:

Love is patient, love is kind. It does not envy, it does not boast, it is not proud. It is not rude, it is not self-seeking, it is not easily angered, it keeps no record of wrongs. Love does not delight in evil but rejoices with truth. It always protects, always trusts, always hopes, always preserves. Love never fails. — Corinthians 13: 1-8

Is Your Marriage Prepared to Survive a Crisis?

Crises are the furthest things from the minds of newlyweds. All they see are bright shiny trouble-free futures. This is as it should be. If engaged couples could get any kind of a glimpse at all of the trouble and woe ahead, they would likely give up on the idea of marriage.

The problem with being blind to the future, though, is that it causes most to be ill-prepared to deal with crises. Unfortunately, crises will come sooner or later. Everyone one day has to deal with the deaths of friends and family members. Health problems of all sorts present themselves eventually. Job losses, forced moves, and financial problems can all befall marriages. Just by living life, problems come and go. Some are minor, some are major. But, one thing is clear, if you live long enough you will encounter some problems that you cannot fix.

It is our response to these problems that makes such a major difference in marriage. Couples who are happily married for a lifetime come to know how to handle crises successfully. Partners also become familiar with how their mates handle stress and how best to support him or her during the crisis.

Much of this knowledge comes from experience. The reason for this is because none of us really know how we're going to handle a major crisis in our lives until the time comes. The good thing is that we can prepare enough so that when a crisis does present itself it doesn't destroy the marriage.

The first thing a couple can do to prepare is to talk about how they have seen other people handle crises. In these discussions you can look to acquaintances, friends and family members. Talk about the severe problems you have seen these people suffer. In particular, identify ways they handled the stress of the situation. Ask yourselves these questions.

26 Ways People Respond to Crises

Did they:

  A. Seek out a friend or family member to talk to

  B. Refuse to talk

  C. Blame themselves

  D. Blame someone else

  E. Withdraw from friends and family

  F. Drink excessively

  G. Take mood altering drugs (illicit or prescription)

  H. Escape (in one of the too many ways to list!)

  I. Seek counseling

  J. Get philosophical

  K. Go into denial

  L. Exercise excessively

  M. Diet excessively

  N. Eat excessively

  O. Pray

  P. Get educated about the problem

  Q. Seek the best help available

  R. Support friends and family

  S. Have a nervous breakdown

  T. Get depressed

  U. Get angry

  V. Leave

  W. Act like a Pollyanna

  X. Work excessively

Y. Talk excessively (beat the problem to death)

Z. Cry (appropriately or excessively)

Once you have talked about some ways people you know have handled their crises, have a talk about how the two of you handle stress. Identify some of the problems you have encountered in the past and what you did to get through them. Then ask each other this question: "How can I best support you when you are going through a very difficult time?"

Love Potion #44

Develop a personal style of saying hello and good-bye to your spouse. Be sure to stop doing whatever you're doing when you say hello and good-bye, and go over to your mate and make loving contact in your special way. Taking the time to do so makes a powerful nonverbal statement that your spouse is extremely important to you.

The Second Biggest Shock

The first biggest shock in marriage comes when you find out that your spouse is not the absolutely wonderful and perfect person you thought you married. Eventually all couples get hit with the second biggest shock of their marriage, too: the realization that they are actually going to have to consciously do things on a daily basis to help keep the marriage vital.

Unfortunately, there are loads of couples that never come to this realization. They stay oblivious to this fact even after their divorce. These are the ones that hold on to the myth that if you are "in love" everything else will come automatically. Wrong! Even in early romance couples put an enormous amount of effort into making the relationship flourish. It was an everyday task. It worked so well it ended in marriage. It may have seemed to come automatically, but in reality a great deal of effort was put in by both partners to satisfy the other's needs in every way possible.

After the early years of marriage are past, the every day tasks of making a living, running a household and raising a family take the place of the romantic activities that keep love alive and satisfying. Even though couples are told this over and over again, it does not sink in. Or, they don't adjust their actions accordingly.

There are several reasons why. Some couples hold tight to the belief that "if we are in love, then everything else will come naturally." These same couples often also believe that if a lot of effort needs to be put into the marriage, this is an indicator that the marriage is not a very good one and is not worth saving. Couples that maintain this attitude usually end up in divorce court or a loveless marriage.

Other couples pay lip service—they agree wholeheartedly but in silence think they are exempt. At least one of the partners considers him- or herself fortunate because his or her own needs are being met, and therefore all is well. Having to actually plan and carry out activities to keep love alive, they think, is for those poor unfortunate people who have lousy marriages. Those that hold this view are in for a really big shock. Hopefully they will come to realize that they too must consciously work on their marriage every single day before it is too late.

Still others have heard the cliché about marriages being hard work, but they think that's really all it is, just a cliché. What these people often think is that making a living and raising children are much more important. They likely wouldn't admit it even to themselves, but doing things to make the marriage work isn't even on their list of priorities. After their divorce, these people often lament, "I just don't understand it. I worked myself to death (at careers or child-rearing). I thought everything was just fine. I mean, sure, we had some problems, but I made sure that the important stuff was taken care of. Then, all of a sudden, out of nowhere my spouse said he/she wanted a divorce and that it was my fault. Go figure!"

Happily married and stable couples go through the shock that love is not automatically "forever." Then they get over it. When they recover, they realize that they need to add activities of love to their daily list of priorities. At the same time, they come to realize that it's crucial to put these plans into action regardless of work, household and child-rearing demands. The couples that do so bypass the heartbreak of divorce and stay happily married for a lifetime.

Love Potion #45

Surreptitiously, look through some picture albums containing pictures of your spouse when he or she was a child. Pick out your favorite one and have it enlarged and framed. You might even consider having it blown up into a poster (most photo shops can send pictures away and have this done for you). Surprise your spouse with the gift. Tell him or her why you liked that picture so much.

The Ten Commandments of a Happy Marriage

Upon seeing the title of this chapter, you may have thought something like, "Oh good. That's what we need—a good summary of what we should and should not do in our marriage." If so, I agree. It is a wise thing for couples to have some rules and guidelines to go by. This is especially true if both people are aware of and committed to following the same set of rules.

To live without rules is to live in chaos. To live in chaos leads to divorce or loveless marriages. In enduring and happy marriages, there are always rules that the couples have committed to follow. Many of these couples have never spoken of these rules, but know what they are.

As vital as rules are to long-term happy marriages, I highly recommend that couples identify, negotiate, write down and commit to the rules they want to govern their marriage.

Having this set of rules helps marriages in several major ways. First, when temptations present themselves as they always do, you will have already had a set of guidelines with which to decide how to act. This is important, as often times temptations can be almost irresistible, especially when you're feeling distant from your spouse. If you have a set of clear rules that you have solidly committed to, it is much easier to "just say no."

Second, when partners take the time and effort to identify and commit to a set of rules to live their marriage by, it solidifies the relationship. Relationships benefit tremendously any time the partners take an action that expresses commitment for a lifetime. Verbalizing this commitment through rules provides your partner with a great deal of security and helps love to endure and flourish.

Third, making written and spoken commitments to another person creates individual pride and strength. Again, this is important for meeting the challenges of temptation. Some temptations in life are so strong that they take a lot of will power to overcome. Commitment to a clearly defined set of guidelines can give you the boost of will power you may need to meet such a challenge. And, as human beings, once we make commitments we are very reluctant to break them. This is especially so if they are commitments of our own making.

Fourth, commitment to a set of personal marital commandments will help you treat your spouse in loving ways even when you are tired, stressed out, irritable, depressed, angry, cranky or feeling unloved. It is much easier to be a loving spouse when you're feeling great and all is well than to act in loving ways when you're down. It is during the bad times that having a set of guidelines for acting appropriately can really help. They can make the difference between asking for a hug or some "alone time" and screaming and assigning blame.

Fifth (and last), having a strong set of identifiable guidelines will make your marriage a great model for any children you may have. Having and following your set of marital commandments will clearly show your children that both of you are totally committed to making each other feel capable, appreciated, respected, intelligent, sexy and attractive. In so doing, you can be assured that your children will go out in the world looking to establish a similar relationship, one in which they can also become happily married for a lifetime.

Love Potion #46

Plan a weekend get-away to one of your favorite spots. Take a notebook with you. During the weekend, brainstorm different ideas that each of you might like to see incorporated into your personal Ten Commandments of Marriage. Feel free to flip through this book to help give you some ideas. Before the weekend is out, identify, negotiate and write out your set of marital commandments. When you get home, use your creativity to display them for all to see. (Hint: We as human beings are better able to stick to our commitments if everyone around us knows what we have committed to).

Why Fun is Critical to Happy Marriages

When couples first fall in love, one of the major factors that causes the love to flourish is fun. Couples in love have lots of fun. They can't wait to get together. Both planned fun and spontaneous fun are big parts of early love relationships. It isn't surprising, then, that couples who have enduring, happy marriages do the same. Conversely, one of the major complaints among troubled couples is that the fun has drained out of the marriage.

Think about this for a moment. What was your courtship like? Did you look forward to being with your lover? Was there perhaps even the child-like feeling that you could hardly wait to get together? Did the two of you plan lots of outings together to do things you loved? Did you laugh a lot and have a great time? Did you even joke around about common everyday things? Were you comfortable being silly with each other?

If these questions evoke positive responses, then you are among the vast majority. Fun is a big part of the early stages of love. In fact, one of the main reasons people fall in love is the way they feel when they are together. How people feel when they are with their spouses also has a major bearing on the happiness and endurance of the marriage.

All of the current research into love and happy marriages bears out the fact that there is a direct relationship between love and fun. Couples who have great marriages kid around with each other on a daily basis and plan for fun time on a weekly basis. It would follow, then, that a couple who wants to have a happy and enduring marriage will do the same.

Unfortunately, having fun is not so easy. Oh, it's easy enough in early love—it flows naturally. But then work, community commitments, household chores and child-rearing start to take precedence over fun. This too is a natural process. The trouble is, when the fun goes, love also starts to fade. As fun drains out of the relationship, so do the good feelings. When the good feelings are gone, partners often look for someone else to have fun with.

Having fun, then, is a critical ingredient for a happy marriage. And it does not come automatically. It must be planned for and insisted on, and must, of course, happen between the partners. Having fun individually with family and friends is great, but it does not count toward making love prosper.

Love Potion #47

Working individually, make a list of the fun things you like to do. Review the fun things you did together before you got married and write them down. Remember the fun things you did when you were a kid and write some of these down. Consider all the things you have always fantasized about trying out and write some of these down. Also, include fun activities that don't cost any money as well as every-day fun things like hugs, compliments and jokes.

Once you both have a list made up, trade lists. In the next month, take the responsibility of taking three things off your partner's fun list and put them into action. Take pleasure in doing some of the fun things your spouse likes to do even if they aren't exactly your types of fun. As an extra, plan to put some fun into your sex life.

One caution. During the fun times, agree to not deal with conflict. Dealing with conflict is necessary in a marriage, but it also ruins fun. So deal with conflict at other times and lay it aside when you are out having fun.

Do You Say Yes—or No—Too Much?

Some people say yes too much. Some people say no too much. Too much of saying yes can be harmful in a marriage if it means you're frequently giving in regardless of your own wishes. Too much of saying no can be harmful in a marriage if it means you're frequently resisting the wishes of your spouse.

Whether or not either partner is either saying yes or no too much is easy to detect in a marriage. All you have to do is to look at the level of satisfaction and types of complaints being made. If one spouse is getting his or her needs met while the other isn't, then there could be a problem. One person may be relenting or denying too much of the time.

A verbal symptom of either is when one of the partners in the marriage starts to complain that his or her needs are not being met. If this is the case, the complaints are normally frequent and persistent. It is important to keep in mind that the complaints may or may not be verbalized between the spouses. If they aren't, the complaints may be made to a third person, or they may be persistent in a person's self-talk.

Normally, though, what happens when one person's needs are not being met is this. First the person subverts his or her needs in favor of satisfying the needs of his or her spouse. This is done in the name of love. After a while, the person starts to assert some of his or her own desires. If these needs are consistently denied, then the person is likely to complain. If the complaints are not resolved, the person will continue to complain.

As the complaints escalate, the expression of the complaints may change. For example, they may come out as a passive aggressive act, a martyr complex or persistent nagging and complaining. While unmet desires and needs are expressed in a variety of ways, one thing is consistent. That is, if one person in a marriage does not feel like his or her needs are being met, sooner or later the love will drain out of the marriage.

Usually when this happens, the other person in the marriage is oblivious. Despite messages from the partner, he or she will think everything is fine—after all, his or her own needs are being met. In marriage counseling these partners say things like, "Sure, I knew we had a few problems, but I just didn't think they were that bad. I mean, my spouse complains sometimes, but I thought we had resolved all that. I just don't see what the big problem is."

By the time couples do come in for marriage counseling because one of the partners feels his or her needs are being unmet, it is difficult to turn around. The complaining spouse often feels hurt and neglected. He or she definitely does not feel capable, appreciated, respected, intelligent, sexy and attractive. It is likely, too, that this person does not hold much hope that meaningful change can or will be made. Compounding the problem is the likelihood that this person no longer feels any love. If this is the case, then the motivation to do the work necessary to turn the marriage around may be low.

Couples who stay happily married come to find ways to satisfy both their own needs and the needs of their partners. They also come to realize that needs can and do change over time. Therefore, in order to keep their marriages vital, they must identify and satisfy these needs.

In doing so, a fine balance must be struck. On the one hand, mature, mentally healthy people take responsibility for knowing and satisfying their own needs. On the other hand, in mature and mentally healthy marriage, the partners learn to identify and satisfy the needs of their mates. The common theme in both cases is that it is essential for the needs of both partners to be met at some basic level.

This does not mean that all needs and desires must be met at all times. This is unreasonable to expect. It also does not mean that each partner in a marriage will have similar levels of satisfaction at the same times. To the contrary, it is perfectly normal in a marriage for one person to be really satisfied while the other is discontented. This is common in a marriage and is not cause to run to the divorce courts.

However, when and if this disparity in satisfaction levels exists, it is imperative that the couple discuss the needs of the person who is feeling dissatisfied. In fact, many discussions may be required to help this person clarify feelings, thoughts, possible plans and goals. To either not talk about it or to limit the discussion to one or two conversations will likely lead to continual dissatisfaction.

However, a sincere effort on the part of the both partners to help each person have his or her needs met goes a long way toward keeping a marriage together and happy. This way, if one partner becomes dissatisfied, he or she feels the support of the spouse. This kind of support and commitment is what cements marriages for a lifetime.

Love Potion #48

Help your spouse do a needs assessment. Ask your spouse to go through the following inventory and to rank each item with either an "ES" for Extremely Satisfied, an "S" for Satisfied, or an "NI" for needs improvement. When he or she finishes, go over each item and ask why he or she answered in that way. Focus just as much on the positive areas as the negative. In the weeks to come, discuss how unfulfilled needs and desires can be better met. (Hint: When discussing the areas that need improvement, no blame should be assigned or assumed. The rule to remember is to give information without blaming and to listen to the information without getting defensive).

The Happily Married for a Lifetime Needs Assessment

Instructions: Rank each item in this manner. If you feel like your needs are being well satisfied in an area, rate it "ES" for Extremely Satisfied. If you feel, on average, satisfied in this area, give it an "S" for satisfied. If you feel likes your needs are not being met in this area, give the item an "NI" for needs improvement. (Hint: Keep in mind that rating something with an "NI" does not mean that you are blaming your spouse; nor does it mean that you are placing the responsibility on him or her to fix the situation).

_____ 1. Laughter and Joy

_____ 2. Romance

_____ 3. Honesty

_____ 4. Gifts

_____ 5. Appreciation

_____ 6. Expressions of Caring

_____ 7. Verbal Affirmations and Compliments

_____ 8. Household Chores

_____ 9. Financial Management

_____ 10. Generosity

_____ 11. Flexibility

_____ 12. Listening and Understanding

_____ 13. Respect

_____ 14. Forgiveness

_____ 15. Security

_____ 16. Intimacy

_____ 17. Playfulness

_____ 18. Respect

_____ 19. Shared Vision for the Future

_____ 20. Support

Please Note: The *Happily Married for a Lifetime* Needs Assessment is a wonderful tool for couples to use to bolster their marriage. However, it can spark blame and defensiveness. If these issues come up for you, either put the assessment aside for another time or consider seeing a marriage counselor to help you work through the issues that come up.

What You Focus on Is What You Get

In the early stages of love, partners do all the right things to make sure that their mates' needs are met. On a daily basis, they go out of their ways to make sure each feels capable, appreciated, respected, intelligent, sexy and attractive.

One powerful way they do this is by focusing on their partners' positive traits and openly admiring them. Things are frequently said like, "You are so considerate. You have such good manners and the things you do make me feel very special"; or, "You're so outgoing. You are truly a joy to be around. Your energy is infectious!" Those kinds of comments help to fertilize the love at hand.

They are so powerful in building a strong foundation of love between two people that I would like to dissect them so we can look at them in detail. In doing so, it is evident that the person giving the compliment first takes notice of some behavior. Next, the person interprets the behavior to be positive. Then the behavior is attributed to a trait the person has. This trait is also interpreted as positive. All of this information is formulated into a compliment that is expressed. In sum, compliments from start to finish look something like this:

A. A behavior or set of behaviors is noticed

B. The behaviors are interpreted as positive

C. The behaviors are attributed to a positive trait

D. The above information is formulated into a compliment

E. The compliment is expressed in a warm and wonderful way

As powerful as this process is to facilitate the growth and maintenance of love, couples tend to stop using it after a while. Then the process transforms. It is not a conscious shift but a major change of focus. That is, for a number of couples, once their needs are not being met, they start interpreting behaviors in a negative way. Then, they attribute the behaviors to negative traits and point this information. The process is the same, but negative. It looks like this:

A. A behavior or set of behaviors is noticed

B. The behaviors are interpreted as negative

C. The behaviors are attributed to a negative trait

D. The above information is formulated into a criticism

E. The criticism is expressed in a cold and contemptuous way

The interesting thing is that the same behavior can go through the compliment process in the early years of love and through the criticism process later on with completely different results. Let's take friendly socializing behavior, for example. When in love this behavior is likely to go through the compliment process and come out something like, "You sure kept everyone entertained at the party. I admire your ability to mix with people and to make friends." But after a few years of marriage, this same behavior may come out something like, "You didn't pay any attention to me last night at the party. All you care about is making friends. You are so self-centered!" The same information was noticed, but the resulting assessment and expression are different.

The reason for the dramatic difference is the focus. In early love, the focus is on the positive. For some couples, at least one partner may change his or her focus to the negative. One reason is because the person feels that his or her needs are not being met and will then strike out with criticism, thinking this will somehow get the other person to meet his or her needs. The thinking here is not conscious, but it is a very real processes nevertheless.

In another marriage, one of the partners may retaliate for perceived criticism. Still others shift from compliments to criticism because that's what they grew up with.

But when it comes down to it, it doesn't matter all that much why people change their focuses. What matters is that they become aware of what they are doing and that they change back to focusing on the positive.

It is critical to the survival and maintenance of a happy marriage that partners interpret each other's actions in a positive way and that they attribute them to positive qualities. To do so is to reinforce both the qualities and the marriage. To do the opposite is to undermine a person's self-esteem and the whole foundation of the marriage. Simply put, all the research says that people will not stay in a marriage if their partners are continually criticizing them.

The research done by Dr. John Gottman at the University of Washington on 2,000 couples also clearly shows that for marriages to be happy, the couples need to have at least five positive exchanges for every negative one. The more positive exchanges you have with your spouse, the more stable and happy your marriage will be.

Love Potion #49

Look over the following list of traits that can be used to label behavior. The list on the left contains the positive and the list on the right the negatives. Make a commitment to yourself to focus on the positive when it comes to behavior that is open to interpretation. Practice on your spouse, your children and friends. (Hint: The more you do this for other people, the more they will do it for you. However, to be effective, give your compliments without thought to reciprocation of any kind).

Kiss and Tell: Part Three

Here is a third set of questions designed to help partners get to know each other on a more personal and intimate level. There are very few things you can do to strengthen a love relationship that are better than spending time getting to know each other's innermost thoughts. Enjoy!

Here are the instructions again. If you wish, change them to suit your purposes and relationship, especially if it will make the process Kissing and Telling more fun.

Kiss and Tell Instructions:

1. Flip a coin to see who goes first. The winner decides whether to Kiss or Tell first.

2. The Kisser gives the Teller a kiss (preferably passionate) and picks a question to ask.

3. The Kisser listens following The Rules of Listening (see the chapter "The Art of Arguing: Part One").

4. The Teller answers all the questions to the best of his or her ability.

5. Switch roles. The new kisser can choose to ask the same question or a different one.

6. Keep a sense of humor and use it often. Laughing and all forms of encouragement are strongly suggested.

Positive Traits	Negative Traits
Modest	Thin-skinned
Grateful	Brash
Agreeable	Childish
Self-defacing	Controlling
Gratuitous	Impractical
Placating	Boring
Sensitive	Over-generous
Forthright	Argumentative
Playful	Cocky
Logical	Gullible
Creative	Stick-in-the-mud
Dependable	Nosey
Giving	Motherly
Persuasive	Belligerent
Self-assured	Know-it-all
Trusting	Perfectionist
Careful	Manipulative
Interested	Withdrawn
Soothing	Impulsive
Direct	Stupid
Assertive	Air-head
Intelligent	Crazy
Exact	Out of touch
Loving	Weak-willed
Thoughtful	Over-bearing
Spontaneous	Inattentive
Imaginative	
Good-natured	
Wise	
Friendly	

Kiss and Tell Questions: Part Three

1. Are you open to taking risks? If so, what kinds, and what is the biggest chance you have ever taken?

2. Remember a time when I was very upset. How did you feel when I was so upset?

3. Are you open to learning more about sex? If so, what do you think we could do to learn some new things?

4. What is one thing you think we could do to improve our sex life?

5. What would you do if you won a million dollars?

6. What do you like about your job? Dislike?

7. How long do you think you will keep your present job?

8. If you could do anything, what would it be?

9. What are the best three things about having sex with me?

10. What is the most eccentric thing about you? About me?

11. What do you want to do when you retire? At what age do you want to retire?

12. Where would you want to live when you retire?

Love Potion #50

Starting tonight, every time you get up from watching television, make sure you ask your spouse if you can get him or her anything. Make a habit of doing it without exception. It doesn't even matter if the answer is always no. Just by asking you will be communicating your love.

Kiss and Tell: Part Four

It's time to play Kiss and Tell again. If you have been playing this game throughout the book, you most likely are starting to enjoy an increased level of intimacy in your marriage. If so, please write and tell me about it or about any of the other experiences you have had as a result of reading this book and trying the Love Potions. You can e-mail me at larry@smartdiscipline.com. In the meantime, here are some more Kiss and Tell questions.

Here are the instructions again. If you wish, change them to suit your purposes and relationship, especially if it will make the process Kissing and Telling more fun.

Kiss and Tell Instructions:

1. Flip a coin to see who goes first. The winner decides whether to Kiss or Tell first.

2. The Kisser gives the Teller a kiss (preferably passionate) and picks a question to ask.

3. The Kisser listens following The Rules of Listening (see the chapter "The Art of Arguing: Part One").

4. The Teller answers all the questions to the best of his or her ability.

5. Switch roles. The new kisser can choose to ask the same question or a different one.

6. Keep a sense of humor and use it often. Laughing and all forms of encouragement are strongly suggested.

Kiss and Tell Questions: Part Four

1. How important do you think it is in a marriage to be playful? To you, what kinds of playfulness are okay and what kinds are not?

2. What is one thing you wish you could unlearn? That you wish I would unlearn?

3. Why do you think so many couples get divorced?

4. Do you believe in angels?

5. Do you believe in ghosts?

6. Have you ever had a religious experience? If so, tell me about it.

7. What is the most embarrassing thing that happened to you when you were young?

8. What is your proudest memory from your childhood?

9. Who is your favorite cartoon character and why?

10. What do you wish you could understand better?

11. If you had a gift certificate from the mall for $1,000, what would you buy?

12. What did you always look forward to doing with your family?

Love Potion #51

Give your spouse a gift certificate for a massage. Better yet, take a class in massage together and practice on each other. You might even want to buy a portable massage table and keep it at home. Imagine soft romantic music, candles and scents. Take turns on separate evenings. Make it so the one being massaged can totally relax and not have to be responsible for anything other than relaxing after the massage.

There are lots of possibilities to give and receive love in Love Potion #51. I haven't met anyone yet who wasn't absolutely delighted with a good massage!

How to Change Lousy Communication Patterns

Good communication is central to being happily married for a lifetime. It is through good communication patterns that our spouse may well come to feel capable, appreciated, respected, intelligent, sexy and attractive. Or, if communication patters are lacking, he or she may well come to feel incompetent, disrespected, dull, unappealing and unattractive. One way of connecting with your spouse will lead to a great marriage and the other to either a loveless marriage or the divorce courts.

The path then to a great marriage would seem simple. Do a good job of communicating and marital bliss will be assured. This is true for the most part. Or, at least, good communication provides one of the building blocks of a great marriage. Of course, the trouble comes in carrying out the task of communicating in such a way that both you and your partner end up feeling capable, appreciated, respected, intelligent, sexy and attractive. While the intentions to do so can be sincere, putting those intentions into practice can be a bit tricky.

Here are some ideas that should help. They are solutions to typical communication patterns that can lead to severe marital problems if they aren't corrected. Please keep in mind as you look over and employ these strategies that you are only in control of your own communication patterns. Do not make the mistake of pointing out the errors in the way your spouse is communicating. While it is okay to give information about how his or her talking to you makes you feel, it is not okay to instruct your spouse in the ways of proper communication. To do so will likely come across badly and will be counterproductive. The very best way to help your spouse communicate more productively is to do so yourself.

Here are the typical communication problems and their solutions.

Communication Problem: Stuck in an extreme negative feeling

Solution: Postpone talking about the issue with your spouse

Sometimes human beings lock onto a negative feeling. When they do, everything they say is likely to flow out of that feeling. One example is jealousy. Jealousy very often is felt intensely. For as long as a person is feeling an intense emotion like this, much of what the person says will be colored, even directed, by the feeling. This is not good. All of the current brain research says that when people are feeling intense emotions, access to the logical side of their brains is cut off. This means the person is acting purely on emotion.

When a person is stuck in a negative feeling like this, he or she is likely to say things that will be damaging to the relationship. Also, the person is likely to say and do things that will only escalate the fight.

The solution to this problem is to recognize when you are stuck in a negative feeling and to refuse to allow yourself the luxury of talking with your spouse during this time. The best thing to do is to talk with a friend, counselor or family member about your feelings. Talk with anyone who is willing to let you rant and rave and get it all out. Once you have done so, give it a little time to make sure you are no longer in the grip of the emotion before you talk with your spouse.

Communication Problem: Moaning and groaning, nagging

Solution: Don't do it, get some help

If you are one of the people in the world that complains about anything and everything, stop it! It will ruin your marriage and your life. For as long as you are complaining, your life will be unmanageable and unhappy. Most complainers picked up this bad habit in childhood and have continued into their adult life. This is too bad, because people do not like to be around someone who is always complaining.

Unfortunately, this is not an easy habit to break. Chronic complaining over time becomes deeply ingrained in a person's life. It becomes the chief way the person deals with his or her world. To change this habit, it will likely take some outside help from a therapist. So, if you have this problem, go get some help. Until you do, you and everyone around you will be miserable.

Communication Problem: Getting angry or frustrated and leaving

Solution: Take a break

Some people, when they get angry or frustrated in a marital argument, walk out. They deal with their negative emotions by physically withdrawing.

If this describes a communication pattern of yours, instead of walking out, take a break. When you are calm and feeling good, explain to your spouse that when you get angry or frustrated, you get an overwhelming urge to leave. Tell him or her that you realize this doesn't solve anything and often makes matters worse. From now on, tell your spouse that when you start to feel overwhelmed you are not going to leave. Instead, you will inform him or her that you need to take a break from the discussion for thirty minutes, after which time you will be willing to come back and discuss the issue further.

I'm not saying this is easy to do. However, continuing to walk out on arguments will one day lead to either divorce or a loveless marriage. So it is worth the effort to commit yourself to resolving problems between you and your spouse. But give yourself a break. Take notice when you're starting to feel overwhelmed, and take a break.

Communication Problem: Hypersensitivity and defensiveness

Solution: Practice asking questions and clarifying thoughts and feelings

Are you one of the many people in the world who can't stand to be criticized? If you are, then the level of your happiness can be greatly enhanced if you can learn to relate to people in a different way. As long as you allow yourself to get hurt and defensive whenever your spouse expresses a negative thought, your marriage and your own happiness will suffer. Change needs to be negotiated in every marriage. For this change to take place, both partners must be open to discussing problems. This process is thwarted if one of the partners is hypersensitive and defensive.

To change this about yourself takes more than telling yourself that from now on you are not going to be sensitive and defensive. Rather, you will need a plan of action. The best one I know of is to start practicing asking questions and clarifying thoughts and feelings.

It is good to start this practice when your spouse is talking to you about things that are neutral and do not give rise to any feelings. Practice on things like the news or what is happening at his or her work. Ask questions and clarify what your spouse is thinking and feeling. When you get good at it, start doing the same when you begin to feel hurt and/or defensive in a conversation. Practice this on both your spouse and on other people in your life.

Put off expressing your own views and feelings. Instead, focus solely on your partner's views and feelings. When you get good at it, you'll notice that you're no longer so hypersensitive or defensive when your spouse complains to you about something.

This is a very worthwhile thing to do for yourself and your marriage. It will greatly increase your enjoyment in life and your self-esteem. But, this too, takes lots of practice. And during the practice, it is necessary to have patience with yourself and to realize that you will make mistakes.

Communication Problem: Blaming and fault-finding

Solution: Give non-critical information and make a request

When one partner is in the habit of blaming his or her spouse for problems, the level of satisfaction in a marriage is low. As human beings, our egos, our self-esteem and our self-confidence are eroded if someone in our life frequently blames us and points out our faults. If this condition exists in a marriage, one of two courses is typically pursued. The person being blamed will either exit the marriage or will stick in it, refuse to cooperate, and try to make the other person as miserable as he or she feels.

The solution is to reduce your complaints to basic information. Here are some examples.

Instead of: "You never listen to me."

Say: "Right now I don't think you are listening to me. Would you take a moment to sit down and talk with me?"

Instead of: "You are so messy. You have no consideration."

Say: "Your socks are on the floor. I feel angry when you leave them there. Would you please pick them up?"

Instead of: "We are late again and it's your fault."
Say: "We are late. I really dislike being late. Would you please do a better job of being on time?"

The idea here is to reduce your complaint to as few words as possible. Doing this will help you to eliminate criticism and blame, which only serve to undermine love relationships. Just giving information followed by a polite request is much more likely to both get you what you want and to preserve your love.

Communication Problem: Contempt and sarcasm

Solution: Get some help

Here is the truth. You might as well know it. If one of the partners in the marriage shows contempt for his or her spouse, the marriage is in deep trouble. Current research says it will end within three years. This is a 97% certainty, according to research done at the University of Washington. Even if it does survive, if dramatic changes are not taken the marriage will be unsatisfactory for both parties. Truth be known, it will likely be a living hell.

Most likely, such a marriage will take some major help from a marriage counselor to turn it around. For couples to turn this situation around by themselves is extremely rare. Even with help it will take a major commitment from both partners. But getting help and making this commitment is a heck of a lot cheaper financially and emotionally than getting a divorce.

There is one other reason to do what it takes to face and overcome this problem in your current marriages: problems follow people. If you are having this problem in your current marriage, then odds are if you don't successfully address it you will end up in another relationship with the same problem. If you are the person showing the contempt, you will likely end up doing the same in another relationship. If you are on the receiving end of the contempt, you will likely end up in another relationship in which contempt is shown to you. There are always exceptions, but this happens to the majority, even when people swear they won't remarry into the same situation.

One thing is virtually guaranteed. When contempt exists between partners, the marriage will end either legally or emotionally. Just as certainly, in order to save the marriage, outside help must be sought. If your partner won't agree to go with you, then go yourself. But go. Doing so may save your marriage.

Communication Problem: Placating, subverting your needs

Solution: Identify needs and negotiate

In marriages, it is destructive if one person continually gives in to the other in order to keep peace in the family. It's very destructive, in fact. This is surprising to those who do it, because they placate their mates in order to help keep the marriage together. Their fear is that if they do not give in to their mate's wishes, there will be trouble. This fear is so real and so great that they think not giving in will lead to more discontent and perhaps to the demise of the marriage as well.

In reality, placating just reinforces a dysfunctional marital communication pattern, one in which one marriage partner demands, often through an expression of anger, that things be done his or her way, and, in response, his or her partner gives in and subverts his or her own needs. Often, this person rationalizes his or her submission to be for "the good of the family."

Whenever this pattern is acted out, it's reinforced. The demanding person gets into a habit of asserting his or her will through anger or threats. The submissive person gets into a habit of maintaining peace in the family by giving in. A common scenario goes like this:

Wife: I'm going shopping with my friend Sue on Saturday.

Husband: I thought we agreed we were taking the kids to the zoo on Saturday.

Wife: I changed my mind. You take the kids to the zoo. I'm going shopping!"

Husband: I don't think that's fair. I really want us to go as a family.

Wife: Tough. If you don't like it, I might just go shopping on Sunday, too. In fact, I think I will do just that. Now what do you have to say to that?

Husband: That's fine. Whatever you want to do is okay with me.

Or another scenario (to show that I'm not gender biased) might go like this:

Husband: I won't be home for supper tonight.

Wife: Again?

Husband: Yes, again. I have to work for a living, remember?

Wife: Sure, but I thought we might spend an evening together for a change.

Husband: Yeah, right. Why don't you call your mother? The two of you are joined at the hip anyway.

Wife: Okay, okay. I'll wait up for you.

Husband: Don't bother.

In both of these scenarios the anger is quite apparent. So are the threats that the situation will escalate into a painful verbal battle if the conversations continue. In order to prevent this from happening, one spouse gives in. Anything, they think, is better that having to deal with an angry outburst.

This process is destructive in a marriage because one of the partners gets used to having his or needs met at the expense of the other. Love, in such a situation, dies. The aggressive person loses all respect for the submissive person. As for the submissive person, several things happen. Self-respect is lost, needs go unmet, anger builds and passive-aggressive actions are taken.

While it is a loving thing to sometimes subvert your own needs in favor of your mate's, it is only functional in the long term if it is being done as an act of love. If it is being done continually as a means of keeping peace, then the act is destructive to the marriage.

If you are the person using anger to get your way, start practicing subverting your needs to your spouse's as an act of love. Also, make a commitment to finding ways other than anger to express your needs and desires. While you're doing this don't tolerate yourself to use anger or threats in any form in order to get your way.

If you are the placater, practice identifying, expressing and negotiating to get your needs met. This can be tough, as many placaters have low self-esteem and self-confidence. If this is true about you, get some counseling or self-help tapes and books. Follow the suggestions until you get to the point where you can negotiate having your needs met despite the potential for anger and arguments. What can help immediately is to use statements and questions like:

"I understand that you really want to go shopping. I want us to go to the zoo as a family. Do you think we can find some middle ground?"

Or,

"I understand that you need to work late tonight. However, I really want us to spend some quality time together soon. What do you think we can do to make that happen?"

Communication Problem: Third-party complaining

Solution: Complain to your spouse only

It is good to have someone other than your spouse to talk your problems over with. Sometimes a friend or family member can provide both understanding and empathy that can greatly ease your mind and support you. Seeking out and developing a support system outside of your marriage is definitely a wise thing to do. The more people you have in your support system, the easier it will be to face life's challenges.

That being said, there is also a downside to having a good support system outside of your marriage. The problem comes when one or both people in the marriage get into the habit of talking their problems over with other people rather than with their spouses. This is understandable, especially if one of these people is really good at listening and empathizing. It is even more understandable if the spouse is lousy at communication.

When people feel like they need to go outside of their marriages to find solace, trouble lies ahead. One clear danger is that they will fall in love with the person who gives it to them. Another danger is that they conclude that intimacy cannot be had in their marriages and so the marriage is worthless to them.

If you have come to rely on talking problems over with someone other than your spouse, make a commitment to change. Decide to find ways to improve communication patterns with your spouse until both of your needs for understanding and intimacy are met within the marriage. During the time you are doing this, cut your complaining to family and friends down to a bare minimum.

Communication Problem: Throwing in the kitchen sink

Solution: Conscious commitment to do away with blame, fault-finding and bringing up mistakes from the past

One common bad practice in marital communication is when a couple starts to argue and one of the partners brings up every mistake the other has ever made in the marriage. Here is a sample of what I mean:

Husband: Can you please hurry a little bit? The movie starts in thirty minutes and you know how much I hate to miss the beginning.

Wife: Well, you were the one that made us late last week for my office party. So get off my back.

Husband: You know perfectly well that that was your fault, too. I would have been on time but you made me stop off to pick up your dry cleaning. But that's the way it is with you. You have no insight into your own faults. Like the time you made us late for my sister's wedding. We missed the whole ceremony. How embarrassing!

Wife: What does that have to do with going to the movie? That's ancient history.

Husband: It has everything to do with it. You just don't have any consideration for anyone else. You are so self-centered. Like last Christmas. That's a perfect example. I wanted to go over to my brother's, but no, you sat around and pouted until I gave in and went ice skating with you. Thanks to you I caught a cold, but did you care? Not in the least. But why should you? You don't care about anyone but yourself anyway.

This conversation could go on and on like this. At least, until the couple gets divorced.

The common recognizable symptoms of the "throwing-in-the-sink" communication pattern are blame, fault-finding and bringing up sins from the past.

People use this pattern for three reasons. First, they use it in order to get their way. Because of the barrage of negative information, their spouses are likely to capitulate in order to end the barrage. Second, people use it to vent unresolved anger and hurt from the past. Third, it is used simply because it is a pattern learned from their parents.

Whatever the reason for using it, it must be chunked if the couple has any hope of being happily married for a lifetime. To stop it, the person doing it must commit to discussing only the issue at hand. He or she must leave off all blame, fault-finding and bringing up past mistakes. How does a person make these changes? By consciously deciding to be aware of what he or she is saying and mustering every bit of will power possible to maintain self-control. This is not easy, I realize, but to continue to "throw in the kitchen sink" is to condemn the marriage.

Communication Problem: Yes-but-ing

Solution: Listen, clarify and be accountable

Yes-but-ing another person is designed to ward off criticism and responsibility. It is a common pattern in marital communication and it goes something like this:

Wife: Could you please make sure you get home on time tonight? We have to leave for the party by seven.

Husband: Sure, but why are you on my case? You made us late last time.

Wife: Yes, but there was a good reason for that.

Husband: Sure, but you always have a good reason. When it comes to my reasons, they are never good enough.

Wife: Yes, but.....

Husband: Sure, but......

In this conversation, both husband and wife are playing the yes-but game. It leads to nowhere and is clearly a no-win situation. The common elements of the yes-but game are refusal to take responsibility and pointing to past mistakes made by the other person.

To intervene and end this bad communication pattern, it requires the commitment of one of the partners to taking responsibility. Instead of saying yes-but, the person says, "Yes, I will be sure to be home on time. I know how important it is to you that we leave for the party by seven." The elements of this healthy communication pattern are commitment and clarification. In other words, the person clarifies the other's request, agrees to it and acknowledges the importance.

Here are some examples:

Husband: I don't like it when I'm the one that has to put the kids to bed every night. How about you doing it sometimes?

Wife: I appreciate it when you put the kids to bed. It frees me up to clean up the kitchen. However, I hear what you are saying about feeling a bit frustrated with taking the bedtime responsibilities night after night.

Husband: Yeah. Actually, I really like doing it. But sometimes I do get tired of it. Especially on nights like tonight when the kids were so hyper.

Wife: What can I do to help?

Husband: Listening to me helps a lot. I guess once in a while I would like to trade-off responsibilities. You know, me do the kitchen and you put the kids to bed.

Wife: I don't see why not. How about trading tomorrow night? Maybe we could even trade every other night if you want.

To communicate in a more functional pattern takes both partners laying aside blame and defensiveness. These must be consciously replaced with a willingness to make requests, clarify the needs and negotiate a solution that is acceptable to both. It can be done. The keys are willingness and consciousness.

Communication Problem: Guilt trips, pouting and sulking

Solution: Make a request and negotiate without the use of guilt, pouting or sulking

Mothers are famous for putting guilt trips on their children in order to gain compliance. For a husband or wife to use the same method to gain compliance from his or her spouse is dysfunctional. When you examine a typical example of this communication pattern, it is easy to see why.

Wife: What would you like to do this weekend?

Husband: I thought I would go fishing with Joe and Steve.

Wife: You left me alone last weekend. I get so lonely when you are gone, I can't stand it.

Husband: But I went over to my brother's last weekend because you went shopping with your mother. You were only alone for a couple of hours.

Wife: You just don't understand. This house is so big and empty when you're gone. Not only do I get lonely but I get frightened too. If you loved me, you would stay home this weekend and do something with me instead.

Most all guilt trips are identifiable by one person using the words "if you loved me" somewhere in the conversation. Also, one person is blamed for how the other feels. Decisions are then based on guilt. If the person does not get his or her way, he or she will likely pout and sulk in order to further his or her cause.

What a mess! There is no place for guilt trips in a happy, mature marriage. The only solution is to stop them. If you are the person using them, stop it. State your needs and make requests. But leave off the guilt trip.

For example:

Wife: What would you like to do this weekend?

Husband: I thought I would go fishing with Joe and Steve.

Wife: I really wanted to spend the weekend with you. Is there some way we can work that out?

Husband: What did you have in mind?

Wife: I don't know. I would just like you and me to find something to do together. I really don't care so much what we do as long as we are together.

Husband: I like to be with you too. How about I go fishing on Saturday morning and spend the rest of the weekend with you?

Wife: Sounds good to me. Let's make some plans to do something fun.

Is this kind of communication realistic? Sure it is. In fact, these kinds of conversations occur daily in happy marriages. To make them an every day part of your marriage takes a conscious effort to state your needs and negotiate an outcome without the use of guilt, sulking or pouting.

Love Potion #52

Take a risk. Talk to your spouse about something that you have had on your mind but have been reluctant to bring up. Broach the subject with a positive attitude and maintain your positive attitude even if your spouse responds negatively. If the response is negative, resist the urge to cut off the conversation or to strike back. Instead listen and see if you can clarify your spouse's position. If you can do this, you will likely find that your spouse will become much more understanding of your position as well.

The Key to Solving All Marital Conflict

Here is the key to solving all marital conflict. Identify and satisfy the most pressing needs of your spouse. Do this and you will resolve the conflict you are having.

As I write this, I can already hear the cries of frustration and disagreement from so many of you. This frustration and disagreement comes from an assumption that I am saying you should do whatever your spouse is asking you to do regardless of your own needs and desires. But I did not say this, and I did not mean to imply it.

What I meant was that if you are in the middle of a conflict, stop and figure out what need your spouse is desperately trying to get you to meet at the moment. Identify and satisfy this need and the conflict will be resolved. Often, this does not mean subverting your own needs and desires. But it most likely means that you will have to lay them aside for the moment so you can objectively determine what need your spouse is trying to satisfy. This is necessary, because as long as you are focused on your own needs you will not be able to effectively respond to your partner.

The most important key to resolving all marital conflict is to identify the needs of your partner and to clarify those needs to make sure you have it right. Most conflicts can be resolved simply by doing this. By most, I mean at least sixty percent of them.

What it takes to do this is to follow the Six Conflict Resolution Steps:

1. Consciously lay aside your own needs, desires, fears and emotions

2. Stop doing what you are doing

3. Look at your spouse

4. Ask him/her what he/she most needs at the moment

5. Clarify that need

6. Brainstorm and negotiate what needs to be done, if anything

Follow this process and you will resolve the conflict you're in at the moment. Resolving marital conflict is actually as easy as that—except for a couple of things that interfere.

Fear is the major barrier to resolving conflict. The kind of fear I'm talking about is when a person is afraid his or her own needs will not be met. There is part of every person that screams out, "Hey, what about my needs?" This loud voice directs a person away from his or her spouse's needs and on to getting his or her own needs met. What it takes to solve marital conflicts is for at least one person to quell this voice so he or she can focus on the needs of the other.

To quiet your own voice is not always easy. This is especially true if either of three conditions exist. One of these is a pressing need of your own. The more urgent you are feeling a need of your own the more difficult it is to lay it aside so you can listen to the needs of your spouse.

The second obstacle comes from negative feelings and/or moods. If a person is in a bad mood, stressed out, or intensely feeling something like anger, hurt, resentment or jealousy, then listening to the needs of his or her spouse is very difficult.

The third obstacle is most sure to loom large if a person's spouse is in a bad mood, stressed out or is intensely feeling anger, resentment or jealousy. These feelings tend to cause people to communicate their needs in ways that cause their mates to feel blamed, attacked, unappreciated, resentful and angry.

As one of these conditions has a likelihood of existing at all times in any given marriage, it is necessary for at least one of the partners to consciously lay his or her own needs and feelings aside and to lead the partner through the Conflict Resolution Steps. This is critical because as long as both people are communicating from their emotions, the conflict is likely to escalate. When people are stuck in negative feelings they are physiologically cut off from access to the logical part of their brains. During this time they are likely to say all kinds of things that are hurtful and inflammatory. This being the case, someone has to take the lead to set aside emotions so he or she can lead the other back out of his or her own emotions and deal logically with the situation at hand.

This process can take anywhere from one minute to several days. During that time, it is necessary for one person to have patience and to keep cool. It's extremely helpful if that person can give his or her spouse as many messages as possible that he or she is capable, appreciated, respected, intelligent, sexy and attractive. It is also helpful to give direct messages and to make requests like:

> "I love you and I care about you. I want to know what your needs are. Let's sit down and talk about them."

When the person does start to talk, it is likely that you will still have to consciously lay your feelings aside so you can listen. It is helpful to remember that when a person is responding emotionally, he or she is very likely to make statements that can cause a person to feel blamed, hurt and attacked. However, if you can "stay in your head" and not get emotional yourself, you will have a chance to listen to and clarify your mate's feelings and desires. Once this is done, there is a much greater likelihood both of you can calmly and rationally brainstorm and negotiate a solution to the conflict.

Love Potion #53

The next time you notice your spouse is upset, stop doing what you're doing, and say to him or her, "Let's sit down and talk about whatever is on your mind." If you notice yourself starting to feel negative emotions during this process, in your own mind tell them loudly to "STOP AND WAIT!" Do not allow yourself the luxury of expressing your own feelings, desires or needs until you have identified and clarified those of your spouse.

Each time that you do this successfully you will be rewarded in at least several ways. One way is that the conflict will likely come to a resolution much more quickly and easily than if you focus on your own feelings, desires and needs. A second reward will come from your mate's gratitude for responding to his or her needs in a loving way. The third reward will come from a rise in your self-esteem. Every time you consciously control your own emotions, your inner voice will pat you on the back. This is a really good feeling and it builds self-confidence.

Why People Resist Marriage Counseling

Sometimes, if a marriage is to be saved, counseling is necessary. Marriage counseling is especially necessary if either one of the partners has emotionally withdrawn from the marriage, if there has been an affair or if one of the partners is focused on the negative traits of his or her spouse. All three of these circumstances are very difficult for people to turn around on their own. It may not be impossible for them to do so, but the likelihood of success is low.

When it comes to marriage counseling, often one or both of the partners are resistant to the idea. The resistance is usually founded on one of several attitudes people typically have about marriage counseling.

One common attitude is that counseling is expensive and probably not worth the cost. It is true that counseling is expensive. Even if you have insurance to cover it, there is still a chance you'll have to pay up to fifty percent of the cost out of your own pocket. As each session can run anywhere from $60 to $150, this can run into a lot of money. People in counseling average eight sessions, so the out-of-pocket cost if you have insurance could run between $240 and $600. If you don't have insurance it would be double these figures. However, the costs could exceed these figures if you needed to go more than eight times.

But whatever the costs, they are far less than the costs of getting a divorce. Legal costs can and do run into the thousands of dollars. The financial burden of establishing two households is also high. And then, there are the costs of selling off joint assets, which must be considered. Finally, one of the partners will most likely have to pay child-support or alimony. Even if you are on the receiving end of the alimony and child support, it will usually be far less than what is needed to run the household the way it was run during the marriage. Compared to all of these costs, marriage counseling is a bargain.

Another reason why people resist marriage counseling is because they feel like their spouse is only using the counseling as a means of ambushing them. They fear that when they enter counseling the counselor and their spouse will gang up on them to make them out to be the bad person. While one or both people in counseling may try to paint their partners in a negative light, a good counselor will intervene in this process. Nothing is gained in counseling by assigning blame and most counselors are skilled at moving people out of blame and into more productive ways of dealing with the couple's marital problems.

Then too, there is the fear people have that they are being drawn into marriage counseling only because their spouse wants to end the marriage and feels like the counselor can both justify and facilitate this process. If this fear is present, then it should be voiced so the counselor can deal with it directly. It may or may not be that ending the marriage is one of the partner's reasons for entering into counseling. Whether it is or not, it is good to get the issue out into the open so it can be dealt with one way or another.

A closely related issue that causes people to refuse to enter into counseling has its foundation in the feeling that "if you need counseling, then there is no use of continuing the marriage." This is particularly true for perfectionists, who have a need to keep everything in their world orderly, neat and controlled. Marriage is not this way and will never be this way. While this attitude keeps a number of people from trying counseling, it should not. If anything, counseling should help these people satisfy their needs for order, neatness and control.

Some people, when asked by their spouses to enter into marriage counseling, put a condition on their participation. That is, they try to bargain by saying they will only go to counseling if their spouses will guarantee they will stay in the marriage and not seek a divorce. Some spouses are more than willing to make this commitment. If so, that's fine. If they aren't, however, this deal can end the marriage counseling before it gets started. The trouble with this is that the person demanding the guarantee has set up a self-fulfilling prophesy. In other words, by demanding something that his or her spouse is unwilling to agree to, he/she is facilitating the end of the marriage. Anyone with this attitude should back away from it and give the counseling a try. Doing so will at least be giving the marriage a chance at survival.

There are myriad other reasons people resist counseling. They include not wanting to admit failure, not wanting to air "dirty laundry" in front of a stranger and not believing there is a problem severe enough to warrant counseling. All of these reasons cause people to say no to counseling. Instead, they plead with their spouses to "work it out together." Sometimes this can work. If the one suggesting the counseling is agreeable to working the problem out in private, it is wise to agree to counseling should the problems not be worked out by some set future time.

Last, I think the biggest reason people resist marriage counseling is because they are afraid. They are afraid of the emotional pain they might have to go through. They are afraid of the painful things they might have to talk about. And they are afraid to face the changes that marriage counseling might lead to. When committing to marriage counseling, there are many unknowns. It is totally uncharted territory and people enter into it full of fears. This is not an easy thing to do. However, many who take the chance are able to improve their marriages dramatically.

Love Potion #54

Get out of your ruts. Commit to doing one thing differently each day next week. One night sleep on each other's side of the bed, one morning make love, one evening play a game, one weekday evening go out to a movie, one weekend go hiking, one day act on an impulse and one day go dancing. Or do anything you like. But do different things.

Take turns deciding what those things are. Make a commitment to going along with them even if you don't feel like it at the moment. Also, give each other permission to do something different without an expectation that it is going to work out perfectly.

What to Do if Your Spouse Is Addicted to Alcohol or Drugs

Alcoholism and drug addiction destroy families. I know of no other conditions that take more of a toll on marriages. Over my years in the counseling profession I have seen many couples go through years of pain and agony brought on by the behavior that accompanies addictions. Many of these marriages—in fact, most—end in divorce. Even when the divorces take place, the pain and agony don't end. The addicts, once divorced, drink more or take more drugs and their behavior worsens. Much of this bad behavior still affects their former spouse and children.

What I am saying is common knowledge. Actually, most people have personal knowledge of either a friend or family member who is addicted to drugs or alcohol, so they are familiar with the devastation that addiction causes.

In marriage, it is not possible for love to flourish if someone is actively addicted to alcohol or drugs. The couple can pretend for a while that everything is okay but it is not. For as long as the person is using, the marriage is on a crash course with disaster. There may be times along the way that all seems to be normal, even good. But, in both alcoholism and drug addiction, the symptoms always progressively worsen. Even if a person stops for a while and goes back, he or she will quickly return to the former level of usage, then surpass it, just as if he or she had never stopped. This isn't on purpose. It is because that is the way addiction works.

Behavior also worsens over time. It is common for people addicted to drugs and alcohol to have affairs and otherwise act irresponsibly. Some are able to maintain jobs and even act well enough to make extended family members and friends think they are functioning normally. Spouses know better, though. Over time they see first hand that both the addiction and the behaviors are getting worse.

It takes a while to wake up to the fact that a spouse is addicted, though. Initially, a spouse will rationalize the excessive use of alcohol or drugs. He/she may blame it on stress or even pass it off as recreational use. When bad and irresponsible behaviors first appear, these are quickly apologized for and forgiven. Following unusually bad and irresponsible periods of behavior, the addict quite often goes into a period of acting his or her very best.

This process of very bad behavior followed by exemplary behavior drives the spouses a bit nuts. Just at the point when a spouse has decided that he or she can't take it anymore, the addict starts acting his or her very best. During this time a state of euphoria can exist in the marriage. Everything goes so well that all of the bad and irresponsible behaviors are swept under the rug. The partners, in essence, kiss and make up. The spouse also becomes enormously relieved and thankful that all the problems have gone away.

Once all is forgiven and is calm and peaceful, the addict goes back to drinking or taking drugs. This may be several hours, days, weeks or even months later. But assuming that no treatment is sought, the vast majority go back to drinking or taking drugs again. Each time they do so, the usage and the behavior get worse. When these reach an intolerable level for the addict's spouse, the usage will likely stop or lessen to the point that behavior can return to acceptable levels again. Then the cycle starts over. After repeated rounds alternating between periods of good behavior and abstinence and periods of bad behavior and using, the addict will eventually lapse into long periods of excessive use and deplorable behavior which he or she cannot control.

While the addict progresses further and further into his or her addiction, the spouse spends more and more energy trying to fix him or her and all the problems he or she is causing. Eventually, the spouse can no longer deny the problems or fix them. At this point, the marriage crumbles. If it does not end legally, it ends emotionally. The addict is too far into his or her addiction to be able to contribute to the marriage, and the spouse is too busy trying to run the family all alone to contribute. So, the marriage ends.

The only way out of this predictable and damnable scenario is for the addict to stop taking drugs or drinking and to get some help. Rarely can a person beat an addiction on his or her own. Most try and very few are able to do so. Left to his or her own devices, the person will most likely go right back to drinking or taking drugs again.

Even so, most addicts resist getting help. Over and over, they refuse it. This is predictable, because addictions perpetuate themselves. They get such a grip on a person that they cause the person to say and do whatever is necessary to ensure a continual supply of the alcohol or drugs. As treatment is a potential threat to this supply, it is refused over and over again. The addict will make excuses or promise to get help, but when it comes down to it, he or she will not follow through.

It is only when the addict's life falls apart that the person has much of a chance of accepting help. Most spouses unwittingly postpone this from happening by assuming the addict's responsibilities and by keeping the addiction secret from the extended family and the workplace. The intention behind these actions is good. The spouse's intent is to do whatever is necessary to get the addict to stop using and to straighten out his or her life. The periods of no use and exemplary behavior perpetuate the hope that eventually things will be okay. In the meantime, he or she keeps fixing problems and doing whatever is necessary to keep the family afloat.

The best chance for the addict to get help comes when his or her spouse can no longer cover up the problems. At this point either the spouse or the workplace finally issues an ultimatum to the addict to quit and get help. Ultimatums cause some alcoholics and drug addicts to do just that. Others are so in the grip of their addiction that they continue to use and deny help despite knowing that they are going to lose their family or job if they do so.

If the addict does have a chance at getting help, it will most likely come when the family or workplace intervenes. The most effective interventions result from the joint efforts of the family and the workplace. In such a case, the addict is confronted and offered help.

Interventions are best planned, prepared and coordinated by professionals. Usually, by the time the family or workplace is ready to intervene, the addict is a danger to himself or other people. The person may be driving while under the influence and the chemicals he or she is ingesting may be taking a toll on the person physically. Other behaviors may also be endangering the person or surrounding people. If this is the case, it is also likely that the addict is blinded by his or her addiction to these facts. The addiction, in order to enable continued access to the alcohol or drugs, causes the addict to either not recognize or rationalize the problems away.

Breaking through this denial is tough and critical. For the person to get help, doing so must be mandatory. If the addict can find any possible way out of it, he or she will. The addiction causes the person to do so. That is why interventions are best left up to professionals. These are people who are experienced and skilled at helping alcoholics and drug addicts to break through their denial and to accept the offer of help. Backed up by ultimatums from the workplace and family members, professionals have a very good chance of getting the addict to accept help.

If the person you are married to has a problem with alcohol or drugs, you will need to get some help. Do not wait until your spouse is willing to agree to it. By that time it may be too late to save either the person or the marriage. The sooner you get help the quicker you will be able to help stop the devastating effects of the addiction on your spouse and on your family.

Help, fortunately, is readily available. One sure way to find out where to get help is to call a minister. Ministers make referrals all the time and will know places that are supported by both private and public funds. Another avenue of finding help is the yellow pages of your telephone book. If you look under Alcoholism, you will find numbers to call for both treatment centers and Alcoholics Anonymous. Even if the problem is with drugs, these people will know how you can get the help you need.

The good news is that there is help available. Lots of it. And there is help not only for the addicted person but for the spouse as well. One of the best avenues of help for spouses is Al-Anon. These groups are free and filled with people who are willing to help and who are going through the same thing you may be going through. Al-Anon is the sister group to Alcoholics Anonymous. Both are twelve-step programs and have the greatest record of success helping alcoholics and their families.

Whether the problem is with alcohol or drugs, go to one of the Al-Anon groups in your area (they have them virtually everywhere, even in rural areas). These are groups of very caring and knowledgeable people. Some have been through exactly what you are going through. Others will be going through what you are going through at the same time you are. It is a wonderful feeling to talk to people who can relate to you. These people can and will also help you access other avenues of getting the help you need.

Another good source of help is through employee assistance programs. Most large employers provide counseling and referral services that can be accessed by both the employees and family members. They are commonly referred to as EAP's. The personnel department will know the number to call. Even if one is not available through the job site, you can look in the yellow pages under Employee Assistance Programs. All large cities and many small cities have them. As two of the major problems these programs deal with are alcoholism and drug addiction, they will know all of the community resources available. Call and ask. Most likely they will be happy to assist you.

Community mental health centers and hospitals also will be able to assist you. Call either and ask to speak with someone who knows about community resources for alcoholism or drug addiction. You will be put in touch with someone who can help you.

The easy thing is to find help. The tough thing is to reach out and get it. It is tough because if you are married to an alcoholic or drug addict, you most likely don't want to admit it. Getting help causes a person to face the reality and severity of the problems. This is not an easy thing to do. It is painful. However, the best chance of getting the addict help happens when his or her spouse gets some help. Waiting for the addict to get help is to wait too long. By the time he or she does, the problems caused by the person's bad and irresponsible behavior may be unfixable. Like cancer, the earlier addictions can be treated the better the chance of a successful resolution.

Love Potion #55

If your spouse has a problem with alcohol or drugs, look up Alcoholics Anonymous in the phone book and find out where and when there will be an Al-Anon Meeting (these are the meetings for the spouses). Go to the meeting and participate or just sit back and listen. (Hint: These meetings are confidential.) If you go, you may tell your spouse or not. If you decide to tell, be prepared for a negative or even derisive reaction. Addicted people shun anything that threatens their addiction. Regardless, the important thing is to get some help for you. Getting help for yourself is the first step in getting help for your spouse. Until both of you get some help the marriage will remain on a collision course with divorce, either emotional or legal. Death is the only other option.

As I want all of my love potions to be positive, let me end on this happy note. Millions of people get help every day for addictions of every kind. Help is abundantly available for both the addict and the family members. Millions of people are also in recovery from these problems and go on to lead happy and productive lives. Many of them also go on to be happily married for a lifetime.

Every Marriage Needs a Henry Kissinger

All couples have problems. While it is true that some have more than others, conflicts are present throughout all marriages. The couples who go on to be happily married for a lifetime find ways to resolve these conflicts that are satisfactory to both parties. They also address and resolve them before they get out of hand.

Every marital conflict has stages of growth and development. First, someone says or does something that the other person doesn't like. Either it hurts the other person's feelings or it is objectionable to the person for some reason. Second, the offended person decides whether or not to communicate his or her discontent. Some problems are resolved at this stage simply by the person dropping the problem. However, even if the person decides not to communicate his or her discontent, it may fester and come out indirectly.

If the problem gets communicated, the third stage begins. This is the initial response stage. If the problem is clearly communicated to the person, the response time will likely be short. The less clearly the problem is communicated the longer the response will take. Regardless of the response time, the marriage partner makes a decision as to how he or she will respond. This choice will be greatly affected by the way the problem was communicated. If it was communicated in a positive way without blame, then the person will likely have a positive response. The opposite will usually occur if the problem is communicated in a negative manner.

Once the problem has been communicated and an initial response made, the conflict enters into a negotiation phase. It is in this phase that couples identify the way each person would like to resolve the conflict. Each person further clarifies how he or she views the problem, what should be done about it and by whom. Eventually, partners will either come to some sort of resolution or lay the problem aside without resolving it. If the latter happens, the problem will likely arise again and again until it is finally resolved or the couple gets a divorce.

In happy marriages, of course, the problems are resolved in a way that satisfies the needs of both partners. Neither partner, in a healthy marriage, is willing to resolve conflicts in ways that only satisfy the needs of one person. Rather, solutions are found and agreed upon that both people not only can live with, but feel good about.

To enter into the negotiation phase requires that one person in the marriage act the part of Henry Kissinger. That is, someone needs to both initiate the negotiation process and to move it along to a successful conclusion. Certainly both partners have to participate in the process, but one person is going to have to initiate and facilitate the negotiation. This takes one person laying aside his or her own feelings and needs at least for the time being. Until this happens, both people are likely to stay "in their feelings," and chances for resolution will be minimal.

When someone can step into the impartial role of Henry Kissinger, he or she can say, "Why don't we talk about this. Tell me how you are feeling. Tell me what you think should be done." Doing this greatly enhances the chances that the other person will be willing to enter into the negotiation phase. Once in the negotiation phase, chances of a satisfactory resolution for both are greatly enhanced if the partner in the role of Henry Kissinger can first listen to and clarify feelings and the desired solutions of the spouse before proffering any of his or her own.

This is not easy to do because of fear. What gets in the way of the negotiation process is the fear that one of the partner's feelings, needs and desires will be trod upon. But, in happy marriages, at least one person makes the effort to control his or her fears and lays them aside. In essence, this person takes on the impartial role of Henry Kissinger. It is one of wise strength that, when successfully carried out, sends an underlying message that "I care about you enough to lay aside my own feelings and desires so I can listen to yours; you are so important to me that I want to make sure your needs are being met."

Doing this for your partner is a great gift. It is certainly a gift to the other person, but it is also a gift to you. Each time you do it, you prevent blow-ups and you increase the chances of an outcome that fills your needs as well.

In reality, one person in a relationship takes on the role of Henry Kissinger most often. It is like sex. In every relationship, one person most often initiates it. This is not always desirable. As in sex, it is better for the relationship if both people can share the roles. However, realistically speaking, one person will always be the chief initiator. So, if you are the one who most often is willing to take on the role of being Henry Kissinger, be pleased and pat yourself on the back. It is a great role to have in a marriage. It will contribute to the peace, harmony and longevity of the marriage.

Love Potion #56

Establish a nonverbal sign with your spouse that says, "Let's talk. I'm willing to listen to you. Tell me what your feelings and desires are." Try this sign out the next time your spouse is upset about something.

Also, go shopping for a mask of Henry Kissinger. Hide it and wear it the next time your spouse is upset. A little humor can go a long way in settling disputes. Come to think of it, a Nixon mask might work just as well.

Deep-Sixing Self-Fulfilling Prophecies

Self-fulfilling prophecies in a marriage are destructive. It is a process that sets a couple up for the same arguments over and over again. The arguments get worse over time and typically do not end with anything positive for either person. Following is an example of how they get started, how they are perpetuated and how they undermine the happiness of a marriage.

Let's say a husband asks his wife to bring home his favorite ice cream one evening on her way home from work. She agrees. He reminds her not to forget because he wants to have it when he watches his favorite television show that night. The wife tells him not to worry, she won't forget. When the husband's television show comes on, he goes looking for his ice cream but it's not there. The husband asks his wife what happened and she apologetically admits that she forgot the ice cream. Walking off in a huff, the husband says, "I can't believe you did this to me. You knew how important it was to me. I even reminded you." The wife again apologizes. Still, there is a similar incident a couple of weeks later.

Once the same mistake is made a couple of times, the spouse who is offended by the behavior unconsciously makes a decision that this is going to be the way it is from now on. But, nice guy that he is, he decides to give his wife another chance. Almost predictably, she blows it. Both her and her husband expected she would, and she did. When this happens the foundation is laid for the creation of a self-fulfilling prophecy that can wreak havoc in the marriage.

From now on, the husband assumes that his wife is not responsible enough to keep her commitments. Then he starts to act on this assumption. The next week when he wants ice cream, he gets it himself. He also drives across town to pick up his dry cleaning because he needs his blue suit the next day and thinks to himself, "I wish I could get Susan to pick up my suit, but I can't rely on her. She'd probably forget it like usual."

Each time something like this happens, a little more anger builds up.

Then one day the husband makes a remark in the morning about needing to have his dress shoes picked up that day at the shoe repair shop. He mutters under his breath that he just doesn't have time to pick them up but that he really needs them for church on Sunday. His wife then asks him if he would like her to pick the shoes up. He replies no and says that he will do it himself.

Guess what happens next. He forgets. And whom does he blame? His wife, of course. Why? "Because," he says, "my wife is so irresponsible, I can't rely on her to do anything. I have to do everything and I just can't do it all myself. My wife needs to help, but I can't rely on her for anything!"

In essence the wife gets blamed for not doing anything. In fact, she even offered to pick up the shoes and her offer was refused. She points this out to her husband, saying, "I asked you if you wanted me to pick up your shoes and you said no. How in the world am I to blame for you forgetting to pick up your shoes?" He replies, "I knew if I asked you, you would forget. You always do. I can't do it all myself. But I can't rely on you either." What a mess!

The good thing is that self-fulfilling prophecies can be laid to rest so that they do not keep harming the relationship. To get rid of them requires consciously identifying and discussing them.

They are easy to identify. Just watch and wait for them. If they are a part of your marriage, they will show up. When they manifest themselves they will be accompanied by blame, anger and words like, "That's the way you always do it!" and "I knew it. I knew it. That's just the way you are!" Or, "I didn't ask because I knew that's what would happen." When feelings and statements like these are present together, a self-fulfilling prophecy is probably at work.

Once the dynamic is identified, all it takes to begin to abolish it is discussion. Self-fulfilling prophecies are some of those devils that cannot stand the light of day. The very act of talking about them destroys them. To do so, though, you may have to wait until neither of you is intensely angry over an incident surrounding the prophecy.

Love Potion #57

Have a discussion about self-fulfilling prophecies. Ask the following questions of each other:

1. Are you aware of any self-fulfilling prophecies that affect our relationship? If so, what are they?

2. What do I do that annoys you on a regular basis?

3. What don't I do that annoys you on a regular basis?

4. What angers you that you don't tell me about?

Take turns asking and answering these questions. The answers should help bring out any devilish self-fulfilling prophecies so they can be chased off. (Hint: Don't get too serious when asking these questions. Be honest in your answers and non-defensive when you listen to your spouse's answers. And have fun with it. It will be much more curative that way.)

Prayer and Marriage

Which do you think is a better way to predict the level of happiness in a marriage—how many times partners make love or how many times they pray together? By the title of the chapter, I'm sure you know the answer. According to a Gallup poll, how many times partners pray together is a better way to predict marital happiness than the number of times they make love.

In some ways this is surprising and some ways not. On the one hand, you would think the happiest marriages would be the ones in which the partners make love the most. But then, when you think about it, it makes sense that if partners pray together, that means they are a close and loving couple.

When you look at the studies that have been done on love and prayer, a number of other interesting things are revealed. Partners who pray with their spouses: believe their spouses are more skilled lovers (62% vs. 49%); show more respect for each other (83% vs. 62%); agree on child-rearing issues (73% vs. 59%); and are more playful (56% vs. 45%). In addition, while individual prayer correlates with marital happiness, joint prayer correlates at a level twice as high. All of these statistics are from the book *The 30 Secrets of Happily Married Couples* by Dr. Paul Coleman.

Coleman cites a few other interesting facts about prayer and marriage. Couples that have reconciled after one person seriously wanted out of the marriage engage in joint prayer 85% of the time. In the study, other variables among recently reconciled couples were considered as well. These included frequency of sex, equality viewpoints and conflict resolution skills. While each of these had a bearing on successful reconciliation, none had the effect of joint prayer.

According to another Gallup survey, marital stability and happiness are affected by the religious involvement of couples of all ages. According to research reported in the *Journal of Marriage and the Family*, the happiest marriages are the ones in which the couples are highly involved in religion.

Just why partners that pray together stay happily married has not be established. However, research by priest and sociologist Andrew Greeley found that there is a correlation between partners' passion for religion and the passion they have for each other. In his research, he established that the more involved partners were in their religious life the more likely they were to report satisfying and intense sexual relationships.

Other research reported by Dr. Larry Dossey in his book *Recovering the Soul* establishes a direct relationship between prayer and healing. What is interesting about his studies is that they scientifically verify a relationship between healing and prayer. As all love relationships are in need of healing at one time or another, this is good to have verified.

The message of this chapter and of all these studies is that prayer and religious involvement enhance marital stability and happiness. Most, I would suspect, intuitively already know this. But it is good to have it verified. And good to be reminded of it as well.

Love Potion #58

Consider starting your day off together reading from a daily devotional book. Most religions and denominations have them. Or you can find them at both regular and religious book stores. Starting your day together in prayer can help you be more cheerful, hopeful, energetic, decisive, reliable, tender, open and loyal. Sounds like a good way to start your day, doesn't it?